CHASING DENALI

The Sourdoughs, Cheechakos, and Frauds behind the
Most Unbelievable Feat in Mountaineering

JON WATERMAN

Guilford, Connecticut

ALSO BY JON WATERMAN
Northern Exposures
The Colorado River
Running Dry
Where Mountains Are Nameless
Arctic Crossing
The Quotable Climber (Editor)
A Most Hostile Mountain
Kayaking the Vermilion Sea
In the Shadow of Denali
Cloud Dancers (Editor)
High Alaska
Surviving Denali

An imprint of The Rowman & Littlefield Publishing Group, Inc.
4501 Forbes Blvd., Ste. 200
Lanham, MD 20706
www.rowman.com

Distributed by NATIONAL BOOK NETWORK

British Library Cataloguing in Publication Information available

Library of Congress Cataloging-in-Publication Data available

Names: Waterman, Jonathan, author.
Title: Chasing Denali : The Sourdoughs, Cheechakos, and Frauds Behind the Most Unbelievable Feat in Mountaineering / Jon Waterman.
Description: Lanham, MD : Lyons Press, [2018]
Identifiers: LCCN 2018040879| ISBN 9781493035199 (hardcover) | ISBN 9781493058969 (paperback) | ISBN 9781493035205 (ebook)
Subjects: LCSH: Mountaineering—Alaska—Denali, Mount. | Denali, Mount (Alaska)
Classification: LCC GV199.42.A42 W38 2018 | DDC 796.52209798/3—dc23 LC record available at https://lccn.loc.gov/2018040879

♾™ The paper used in this publication meets the minimum requirements of American National Standard for Information Sciences—Permanence of Paper for Printed Library Materials, ANSI/NISO Z39.48-1992.

For Nicholas and Alistair, again.

We have only to follow the thread of the hero path, and where we had thought to find an abomination, we shall find a god.

—JOSEPH CAMPBELL, *The Power of Myth*

The raven chief [Totson] threw his great spear at Yako, but Yako, using medicine, changed the large wave behind him into a mountain of stone just in time. . . . The raven chief was paddling so quickly his canoe struck the second great mountain of stone. The raven chief was thrown onto the rocks where he changed instantly into a raven and flapped to the top of the mountain. Exhausted, Yako fell asleep. When he awoke he was back at home with his new wife at his side. Gazing around, Yako saw the two mountains he had created. There was a smaller one to the west now called Foraker, but the larger one . . . would be called—Denali! The [High] One!

—CHIEF MITCH DEMIENTIEFF, *Denali Sacred Creation Story*

CONTENTS

Preface: The Flagpole

Off the ice-bound McKinley River, amid rolling tundra hills shadowed by the greatest mountain wall on Earth is a final and unlikely forest. Imagine a broad-shouldered man alone in its midst clutching a small tree.

He made his livelihood digging, manhandling, and horsing hard rock out of icy streams and deep tunnels; with his spruce-built pack frame he lugged god-awful loads uphill among miners freighting half the weight, but he never said as much. The man knew that more than any tree, the prickly white spruce furred Alaska like a great green blanket. Here beneath this icebox of a mountain, these trees grew crooked from the goddamned cold—so cold his spit crackled when he hawked it out. He saw many older and surrounding spruce too gnarled out for cabin logs, but for a flagstaff he only needed this young sapling straight and true. It was heavy with sap, but it would lighten up a bit once it dried.

He felled the spruce with a few well-angled swings of his double-bit and then stripped off the branches and the bark by feathering the blade down its length, wincing as he sliced into his bare hand. Now he pulled back on his huge fur mitts and lofted this lumber like a rifle and sighted up it: fourteen feet tall and ruler-straight, almost five inches at the butt, and two and a half inches at the skinny. He opened his other eye and stared up at the mountain many miles above, shaking his head. A banner of snow flew violent-like off the top, and in a flight of fancy he tried to picture the tree cradled in his arms rooted up there where nothing grew, no man walked, and no bird flew. "Holy Christ," he spat again.

Exhausted from the day's long mush to his cabin to freight in salmon for the dogs, he cupped the sap-frozen butt end of the young tree gently over his shoulder and began breaking trail to his dogsled back up the hill first through sugar snow then stumbling and barking his shins in frozen crust, while the tapered end of the heavy tree—skinned naked and pale—furrowed the snow behind his footprints as in the sign of a giant tail-dragging beaver. So he lifted the pole up and bore its weight across both shoulders. His breath hung suspended in odd white clouds as he floundered and plowed up, grunting at his blood-soaked mitt, the wood digging into his shoulders, the boys howling above as they caught his scent.

Cast of Sourdoughs, Cheechakos, and Frauds

William Robert Taylor: "Billy," the youngest of the 1910 Denali team at twenty-seven, was an all-around woodsman, dog driver, and mining entrepreneur in Kantishna (pronounced *Kan-tish-shina*), Alaska.

Peter Anderson: The tall, blonde "tower of strength" team member, forty-three, from Sweden, not yet an American citizen in 1910, of whom little is known.

Charles McGonagall: Forty, ran mail dogsleds throughout Alaska and discovered the crucial, eponymously named pass into Denali where he had poked around for gold before their climb.

Thomas Lloyd: Welshman-cum-Utah sheriff–turned Alaskan mine promoter and rake who, in middle age, led the other three men on the 1910 Denali Sourdough pioneer expedition.

William (Bill) McPhee: Owner of the Fairbanks Washington Saloon and Store; sponsor of the Lloyd expedition.

William (W.F.) Thompson: Editor of *Fairbanks News Miner* and champion of Lloyd.

Dr. Frederick Cook: New Yorker who explored and attempted Denali in 1903 and 1906, claiming to make the first ascent; author of *To the Top of the Continent*.

Robert Dunn: Journalist from New York who accompanied Cook in 1903 and wrote the book *Shameless Diary of An Explorer* about their trip.

Edward Barrill: The assistant Montana horse packer for Cook's 1906 Denali trip who claimed, initially, to reach the summit.

Belmore Browne: Artist and mountaineer who joined Cook in 1906, then returned to attempt Denali in 1910 and 1912; author of *Conquest of Mt. McKinley*.

Hershel Parker: Alpinist and Columbia University professor who coled the 1906 trip to Denali with Cook; during the 1910 and 1912 attempts, he and Browne exposed Cook as a fraud.

Merl LaVoy: The photographer who took a high-elevation picture of the Sourdough Couloir while accompanying Browne and Parker to Denali in 1912.

Harry Karstens: "The Seventy-Mile Kid" who led the 1913 first ascent of Denali's higher South Summit; he later served as the first superintendent of Mt. McKinley National Park.

Hudson Stuck: The never-married "Archdeacon of the Yukon" was fond of boys and organized the 1913 climb; author of *The Ascent of Denali*.

Walter Harper: The youngest son of an educated Irishman and an Athapaskan woman, Walter became the first to step on Denali's South Summit in 1913; he was Stuck's protégé.

Totson: The bloodthirsty Raven, demigod chief from the Distant Time, who tried to kill Yako with giant waves.

Yako: The young demigod warrior on a hero's path, who paddled west, took a girl from Totson's tribe, and turned an ocean wave into Denali, the High One.

Prologue: June 2016

I pulled the balaclava down over my frosted chin, shivering, as the bottom half of Denali fell into shadow. A raven flew past holding wind in its wings and all of the mountain in its eyes. I sat fifty yards from our 14,300-foot medical camp and right next to the dead body of Pavel Michut.

Several days earlier, this Czech ski mountaineer stepped into his ski bindings halfway up an hourglass-shaped snow chute called the Messner Couloir, sixty degrees steep and rising a vertical mile to the 19,500-foot summit plateau. He made three jump turns, caught an edge, fell head over heels, and continued plummeting toward camp—knowing, in his horrified last thoughts, that dozens of climbers in the basin below were helplessly watching him fall—over rocks and cement-hard ice, until he stopped 1,500 feet later, bent and irreversibly broken. Hot sunlight reflected off the snow and burned his skin, slowly dispersing the atoms that made up his forty-five-year-old body into the mysterious universe of our beginnings.

When the clouds cleared below camp the park service helicopter would fly in from sea level and carry his remains out. I stood up and gave a respectful bow to him there on the landing pad that we had stomped out in the snow.

Death on a mountain foils all the best-laid plans. If you repeatedly spend time on Denali, it's inevitable—lacking a near miss or even losing a friend—that you'll witness a fatality or help with a body extraction. This can feel like the height of folly, taking on these great tests only to earn such wretched consequences. To continue amid such adversity, and to counter the perception that climbing is solely a game of risk addiction, committed climbers also depend upon camaraderie, challenge, the beauty of mountains, and inspirational legends to sustain them through both storm and sunshine.

The addiction to risk—with its brain chemistry rewards—never goes away but can be balanced and put in its corner through mastery and judiciousness. Camaraderie often vanishes outside the intensity of expedition life. Beauty can be as elusive as stormy weather in the high ranges. And even the physical challenge fades as oldsters become incapable of their once youthful feats.

With all of these shifting (and, eventually, fading) motivations that explain why I stopped mountaineering, I realized that the truly committed could never really quit. I had embarked upon a life path rather than a sport. I had also been following others who had inspired me, through what the mythologist Joseph Campbell called "the thread of the hero path."

So this is an investigatory tale of the flagpole-carrying Sourdough heroes—Billy Taylor, Pete Anderson, Charlie McGonagall, and Tom Lloyd—whom I once revered. The example of their lofty achievement, along with their endurance and pluck, propelled me up mountains—until recently, when I began questioning whether they were for real. With the insight and skepticism that only aging can confer, I wondered whether I had merely chased idealistic, youthful dreams based upon an illusion. A myth, rather than flesh-and-blood paragons.

Let me explain. Exactly four decades had elapsed since the first time I stumbled up here on the west buttress route with my scout troop from Massachusetts. In that peculiar way in which only young people can commit themselves wholesoulfully, I had found a path that gave my life meaning.

I wanted to climb mountains and run rivers and spend my days on long journeys through remote landscapes because the physical challenge of adventuring appealed to me through the blood, on a cellular level. If I wasn't out in the mountains or planning the next trip, I succumbed to depression—like most climbers do. Life simply seemed meaningless when I was sleeping on a mattress indoors without wind in my face or untracked horizons to explore. I also believed that the legend that I was chasing had everything to do with a value system based on worshipping the wilderness and its mountains.

So I emulated that foursome of long-dead Sourdough miners, who first climbed Denali in 1910. They had launched their expedition over a bet in a Fairbanks, Alaska, bar. With no mountaineering experience, they shouldered a huge pole up a steep ridge, followed by a dicey ice gully, until they planted the pole on top, tied on a big American flag and jogged back down. All in an unbeatable day, unroped, in winter, and on completely unknown terrain.

Even if I was a touch obsessed about these icons, I wasn't isolated in this thinking. "We have not even to risk the adventure alone," as Campbell said in his book, *The Power of Myth*, "for the heroes of all time have gone before us." In my mind, this spoke directly to those nameless Sourdoughs. Their story was respected by mountaineers around the world as an allegory for slaying dragons, pushing to the limit in spite of enormous odds, but still making it back down safely. After their climb, they nonchalantly disappeared back into the wilderness.

Suitably inspired that June of 1976, my pioneer-fired dreams were briefly set back here in this same basin when I saw another corpse awaiting a helicopter, the eighteenth fatality in the mountain's history. Like the Czech skier, it was a needless death that could have been prevented.

While I didn't plan on risk-taking in 2016, as I climbed higher I was preoccupied about turning older. These are the thoughts, I remembered, that you have to process after a mountaineering fatality. Bury these experiences and they'll come back to haunt you. The only alternative, for me, is to learn from them.

So while seeing lifeless bodies on a mountain is provocative and unforgettable, the experience can serve as a safety net for climbing. Because each step you or your friends take comes with consequences. Forty years ago, we made the right decision, as weather deteriorated in the face of my high-altitude headache and nausea, to turn around before the summit. That expedition spurred me into figuring out how to reduce risk on big mountains, let alone launch a career—based on sharing lessons about safety and history—that kept me in the wilds.

Working as a guide, a filmmaker, and a park service ranger, I returned repeatedly. Ill-disposed for government paperwork and uniform dress, I quit rangering and wrote three Denali books (that mentioned the Sourdoughs) to share what I had learned and then continued my career as an adventure writer.

I spent years on journeys sailing, dogsledding, skiing, ice climbing, trekking, sea kayaking, white-water boating, and backpacking. All based upon expedition skills gained on Denali.

Now, nearing sixty, I refused to accept the idea of retirement. Besides, I made my living from these trips, writing about the adventure along with history, culture, and conservation. Rather than rusting, I planned to go out dancing, despite the broken bones and surgeries and arthritic setbacks that come with letting the animal of your body love what it loves. It didn't matter that I had lost some lung capacity and flexibility and strength. By training hard, if I couldn't set the pace or break trail, I could at least keep younger partners in sight. Experience, technique, and knowing how to conserve energy also gave me an edge—or so I hoped on this final Denali trip.

While I planned to stay fit for another quarter century, the thought of celebrating my June 12 birthday on top, on the day that I would become a sexagenarian, seemed like a karmic invitation into disaster. So I kept this fantasy to myself. As in a new relationship, I repeatedly gazed toward the distant summit and declaimed: *No expectations.*

This summer of 2016, as a park service patrol volunteer, I didn't come back to Denali simply to perform rescues. I came to revisit a mountain that had provided an outlet for my passions: laughing with teammates, climbing above clouds smoking below your feet, or lifting snow that fell as fast as we could shovel in tent-burying storms. Also, I returned because I had unfinished business with both the Sourdoughs and Denali itself.

Until recently, I had abandoned mountaineering as if it were part of a past that didn't belong to me anymore. Aging, of course, has a way of directing you onto different paths. But I wanted to change that.

In the years that had passed since my last visit, the culture of climbing had evolved on North America's highest mountain. My teammates were watching movies downloaded onto their cellphones, climbing traffic had nearly doubled, and in good weather, tourist-engorged, scenic-flight planes swarmed the mountain.

Climbers now pay a $365 fee, submit their registrations two months in advance, and carry park service–issued, plastic-bag lined "clean mountain cans" (CMCs) so that their feces can be disposed of in pre-marked crevasses. Only the bravest climbers carry their full CMCs all the way back down the mountain.

All of this, of course, would have been unimaginable to those Sourdough miners 116 years ago. My skepticism about their claim began a year ago while writing about another bizarre Denali legend. After weeks of research, I found that the elderly hero of my story whom I flew out to interview in Seattle was a fraud who never climbed the mountain. I initially believed his incredible tale about the first ascent of the west buttress route because he vividly described a four-foot-tall, broomstick-width flagpole on the summit in 1948. I figured there was no way—uninterested in mountaineering literature and as an out-sider in the climbing community—that he would've known about the pole unless he'd seen it with his own eyes (the famed mountaineer Brad Washburn planted it in 1947 after climbing the long-established Muldrow Glacier Route). Yet, adventure frauds have long made deception into an art—most famously, Dr. Frederick Cook claimed to make the first ascent of Denali in 1906.

The crux of the Sourdoughs' unbelievable story also hinged on a flagpole that they had supposedly planted on the summit. Only one team of climbers, friends of the Sourdoughs, claimed to have seen their flagpole. And no one produced any photographs of this fourteen-foot pole crowning the continent.

As for the Seattle hoaxer, it took a lot of time and research to debunk his claim. I published two stories about his duplicity—turned out he'd seen a picture of the 1947 Washburn flagpole in a book. Of course, he had no pictures from his own climb and while purportedly backpacking crampons all the way up North America's iciest mountain, he made the preposterous claim that he summited without strapping them on.

Throughout that magazine assignment, I realized that Denali still had a hold over me. But it wasn't enough to write about it like a research librarian. I had to return and spent a few weeks up high—maybe even reach the summit and find my own equivalent of the now passé pole-planting and flag-raising ritual.

After ten days on the mountain, slowly climbing up the Kahiltna Glacier, I learned that modern climbers, young and old, were still inspired by the Sourdoughs. Like most icons, they inspired us to dig in deeper and continue, even in the face of great adversity.

Hungry? Well, the Sourdoughs did their climb with just three doughnuts each.

Should we continue without a rope? The 1910 climbers didn't have harnesses and since they didn't know how to belay, they didn't use ropes.

Cold? The infamous miner pioneers deliberately started their climb in winter conditions wearing heavy canvas and wool.

Despite all those who still believed the Sourdoughs, I found a few mountain guides and one park service ranger who thought that the inspirational 1910 climb was too unbelievable to be true. For starters, most every Denali gully, face, and ridge had now been climbed or skied and written up in four different guidebooks. Yet, the Sourdough route has never been fully repeated.

These beginner miners unknowingly introduced the world to fast, "alpine-style" climbing on high-altitude mountains. It was as if they had jumped into the future and skipped all the preliminaries of exploring the approach and route, or learning how to climb, or taking it slow and conservatively working their way up the mountain. Before their blitz, the mountain had never been climbed.

Today, most Denali climbers also avoid the Sourdoughs' intemperate winter climbing strategy. The modern climbing season—blessed by warmer temperatures and Alaska's constant summer light—runs from May until early July. In 1982, during my winter ascent of a spectacular granite ridge called "the Cassin," surviving temperatures of fifty degrees below zero and dark conditions, barely escaping with my life, I found out how tough the Sourdoughs were. Since I needed both hands to swing the axes or grip the rock, shouldering a fourteen-foot pole was unimaginable. I also learned that in the early spring when they made their summit climb, the upper mountain is armored in blue ice and rock-hard snow, raked by frequent high winds backing the meat-freezer cold.

In winter conditions, tropospheric depressions further thin the atmosphere over the North as if the poles of the earth are being squeezed by a frigid vice. While humans thrive at low elevations surrounded by the thick-aired, protective bubble of the troposphere, atop Denali in the dark of winter only a score of climbers have pushed toward the uninhab-itable stratosphere, which extends from 23,000 feet up into outer space. Compounding the tropospheric depression phe-nomenon, winter makes the 20,310-foot mountain a physio-logic 25,000-foot Himalayan peak. Fortunately, a century ago, these four lowland miners knew nothing about high-altitude acclimatization.

In 1910, even experienced alpinists didn't understand how to acclimate to prevent altitude sickness. It took until the latter part of the twentieth century for climbers to learn that gradual adaptation to high altitudes—resting for a few days at each new elevation gained above ten thousand feet—prevents debilitating headaches, lassitude, dizziness, nausea, pulmonary and cerebral edema, or cortical blindness. But the Sourdoughs unknowingly enacted a bold strategy that only the world's most elite mountaineers practice today: climbing from a low elevation to the summit and back, nonstop, in a single day to outrace mountain sickness symptoms, all of which can be cured by rapid descent to a lower elevation.

In the case of the Sourdoughs, they climbed from 11,000 feet to the 19,450-foot North Peak and back in a lightning-fast 18 hours. Or so they claimed.

The north side's Harper Glacier that the Sourdoughs walked across is also known for a venturi-wind phenomenon, created by air roaring through the constricted Denali Pass and funneling downhill with otherworldly, shrieking gales that have repeatedly lifted up, blown away, buried, killed, or severely frostbitten scores of modern summertime climbers equipped with radioed weather reports and state-of-the-art gear.

They left mountain historians precious little to go on, aside from their word. Their contradictory stories and retractions added further confusion. Nor did it help that three of the four were unlettered and reticent pioneers of the North, without diaries or memoirs or children to advance their legacies. While other mountaineers wrote books and articles and snatched a lifetime's worth of bar boasting for lesser achievements, three of the Sourdoughs mostly refused to even mention their climb.

The first time I saw their route, in late May 1983 while traversing over the mountain, streaks of steep, blue ice surrounded the bottom of that final, unrepeated couloir. Seeing it again in June 1993, three weeks out after dog mushing into the Muldrow Glacier from their mining district of Kantishna and having spent a week climbing the knife-edged ridge below it, I couldn't imagine how they made such short work of it all. Their climb had to be a myth.

On my 2016 Denali climb as a park service volunteer, two of my six companions—all half my age—had been here before. We spent a full week acclimating at 14,300 feet, frequently hiking or skiing a thousand feet higher to accustom our bodies to the altitude. We treated, then evacuated, two frostbite victims from our medical tent. We posted daily weather forecasts, advised climbers, played Yahtzee, and read books.

On the day that we left for the 17,200-foot, west buttress high camp, it appeared that no one in the group had anything to prove. Worried about being the pensioner slowing down young teammates, I had trained up to twenty hours a week through uphill running or cross-country skiing in Colorado. Rather than ordinary workouts, I went alone up a cold mountain and repeatedly pushed myself to exhaustion and beyond. Then, week after week—listening to my body—I extended these limits with a tolerance for suffering that I'd learned through decades of conditioning outside the gym. I had to keep up with companions a lot younger than I was.

As the saying goes in Alaskan mountaineering, there are old climbers and there are bold climbers, but there are no old, bold climbers. So those partners (particularly youthful ones) who claim that they don't consider the possibility of dying or getting hurt on a mountain like Denali are climbers whom you should never rope up with. Fear—of falling, being avalanched, hit by a sudden storm, dropping into a crevasse, or contracting altitude sickness—tends to sharpen your focus and make you pay more attention. Still, since vigilance, luck, or all the experience in the world can't stop a falling rock or any number of other random hazards, I had prepared and left a will with my family in Colorado.

I could accept not making the top again. I'd turned back repeatedly because I preferred a hollow sense of incompletion to more frostbitten digits or the prospect of others risking their lives to rescue me. Or worse. Also, this time, as a soon-to-be sixty-year-old, I had good excuses in case I failed.

Complicating matters, on past trips to these uninviting elevations I had been clobbered with headaches, vomiting, forgetting partners' names, battling insomnia, and nearly drowning in my own fluids—regardless of acclimatization. My family ancestry didn't include high-altitude genes.

Fortunately, compared to the Sourdough route, the west buttress is a relative walk-up, given several days of good weather (uncommonly found up high) on Denali. But below the fixed ropes, parboiling in a snow basin that resembles a fry pan, I developed urgent misgivings.

Being towed up at the end of a rope, breathing hard and sweating profusely, felt miserable. Plus, we were queuing up for a mountain that I'd never seen lines on. At least a hundred other climbers were heading up this day.

What am I doing here? I thought. I had two young sons who had tried to convince me that I was too old for Denali. While my role modeling might show them how to deal with their own aging, they would never talk to me again if I didn't come home. This was prompted, of course, by imagining how wrecked the ski mountaineer Pavel Michut's family would be.

Shaken up by these thoughts and sweat soaked at the base of the fixed ropes, I shouted to our unflappable lead Ranger Bob Tomato: "I'm going down." The rest of the team avoided meeting my gaze, as if I had suddenly become the party crasher. Tomato, lithe and thick-lipped, bow-legged like a bull rider from his many extreme ski descents, strode over and looked me in the eye. No one else said a word.

"You feeling okay?" he asked, sotto voce.

"Yeah," I replied, "physically anyway."

In the first week out, tacitly acknowledging that he would lead without sharing leadership, and that I would write about Denali, we agreed to change his name in print to Bob Tomato—which gave him great pleasure. During the two strenuous weeks that I had observed him in action, to my knowledge Tomato had never breathed hard or broken a sweat. Ten days earlier, when our teammate Bobby Cosker had an erected tent snatched out of his hands and blown out of sight down the glacier by the wind, Tomato scooted after it on his skis and somehow caught it a mile away on the lip of a crevasse. To a mountaineer, particularly a guide or a park service ranger, losing a tent to the wind is the NASCAR driver's equivalent of falling asleep at the wheel and totaling a car—a stigma Tomato would never live down. But as a thoughtful leader, he took the whole event in stride, without issuing any reprimand, acting pleased that Cosker's blunder allowed such a brisk and heroic ski rescue. The rest of the team, however, couldn't resist a rejoinder, and thinking of our hapless partner Bobby flying away under a tent held like an umbrella, my hard-hearted teammates began calling him "Bobby Poppins."

Before Tomato switched jobs to what the guiding community referred to as "the dark side," working for the feds as a park service mountaineering ranger, he had completed his guide certification and successfully escorted many clients up the mountain. Under his skilled protocols, we all understood our role as secondary volunteers. To keep the peace, I acquiesced because real leadership is defined by an ability to follow. While repeatedly trying to make this dead-serious bergführer smile, I observed that Tomato was incapable of laughing unless it was at his own joke. As far as he let on, history concerned old dead guys and the sourdoughs were loaves of bread.

Physically speaking, since the altitude didn't slow him down, you couldn't help but wonder whether Tomato had Sherpa DNA. But before I could verify his lineage, a week ago an unfortunate, dawn meeting of a full, yet topless, pee bottle and two sleeping bags had forever banned me from his tent.

There at 15,200 feet, awhirl with clouds, I caught my breath. And Tomato's shrewd leadership skills would prevail yet again. "You can't go down alone," he said. That settled it—as he knew it would. Since I didn't want to prevent someone else from summiting while they accompanied me down, I had to continue up. *This whole climb wouldn't be such a big deal*, I thought, *if my teammates were all thirty years older.*

I clipped on my crampons to the bottom of the plastic double boots as a set of dangerous-looking claws. More than any other piece of gear, crampons are vital to high-altitude mountaineering. The evolution of this tool over the last century—from four-point, iron strap-on creepers to fourteen-point, stainless steel clip-on spikes—explains how climbers have tackled and succeeded on increasingly difficult climbs on Denali. By stomping each spiked foot into the icy steps leading to the crest of the west buttress, our feet stuck as secure as astronauts' Velcro boots to the space shuttle walls.

In my left, over-mitted hand, I clutched a twenty-inch-long ice ax, jabbing its end spike like a trash-picker stick into the snow. Compared to the eight-pound, four-foot-long, hickory-shafted, step-chopping alpenstocks used by pioneers, the fifteen-ounce carbon fiber shaft lanyarded to my wrist was as space age as the crampons. In my other hand, I pushed a jumar—from its Swiss inventors (Ju)gen and (Mar) ti, which locks when you lean back on it and slides as a one-way clamp—up a rope that had been tied down into pickets and permanently "fixed" on the mountain a month earlier by mountain guides. We also tied into one another with our climbing ropes.

Having all of this modern, lightweight equipment might make a high-altitude climb seem more straightforward, but proper use of the gear is not a journeyman's trick. Two of my very fit teammates, Sergeants Jeff Hamilton and Cory Inman, had never climbed Denali. I could only imagine their trepidation. Still, as armed air force pararescue medics, they had frequently deployed to Middle East combat zones more hazardous than a subarctic mountain. But up on the fixed-rope headwall, they neglected to flex their ankles and climb the forty-five-degree slope flat-footed in order to engage most of their crampon spikes, instead of just their frontpoints. Shouting instructions or trying to teach hard-to-learn and less-comfortable techniques mid-climb wouldn't have worked. So they repeatedly frontpointed and kicked their feet straight in, perpendicular to the slope, straining calf muscles while expending extra time and energy—showing how long-in-the-tooth mountaineers can catch their breath amid muscular, young war heroes.

Our packs were made of the same lightweight spectra-nylon used in bulletproof vests. We wore Gore-Tex bibs and jackets that would keep us dry in storms but allow our sweat to pass through ingenious nylon pores. We kept two-ounce packets of easily digested, vanilla or fruit flavored, mucous-consistency "Goo" gel in outside pockets in case of diminishing blood sugar. Fleece gloves under nylon-shelled pile mitts kept our fingers warm.

Seen from the historical context, we were highly evolved climbing machines. In body and mind, we exploited decades' worth of technology and knowledge about the mountain, essentially standing upon the shoulders of those canvas-jacketed, hatchet-handed, creeper-footed Sourdoughs who may or may not have preceded us.

After stomping a monotonous, over-ballasted upward jig all afternoon, we finally crested the top of the ridge, crampons singing like rusty hinges in tight snow, and walked down onto the broad, sloping 17,200-foot basin. With the mercury hugging the balmier single digits, we felt thankful that it was windless—but this could change instantaneously. So without hesitation, as if expecting an artillery barrage, we began digging in.

For several hours, we quarried out large, rectangular snow blocks with aluminum snow saws, then carried and stacked them around our three tents in a towering barricade. These snow walls would buy us just enough time to dig a more bombproof snow cave in case the all-too common, Denali tent-shredding blizzard should hit.

To my surprise, I had an appetite for the disagreeable freeze-dried food. I slept soundly. When I woke up bound tight as Rameses II in my mummy bag with frost fallen from the tent walls melting on my face—feeling as if resuscitated from major surgery—I had no headache. Still, acutely aware of my age because of the stiffness in my joints, or the relentless call of the bladder, I decided to forgo the summit and call 17,200 feet my high point. For the next two days, just strolling a hundred yards on the flats at this altitude left me gasping and contemplating a raid on the emergency oxygen bottles stashed in the nearby rescue cache.

When June 12 dawned, our next-door neighbors—young snowboarders sponsored by The North Face—began singing "Happy Birthday" across the snow-wall fences. Somehow word had gotten out. Although not pleased to be so publicly reminded of my age, I looked forward to one more day of repose in the tent before descending to thicker air.

Unexpectedly, Ranger Tomato then announced—in his dropped "r"s drawl—that I would continue to the summit, escorting our teammates while he and Justin Fraser stayed behind and supervised a helicopter lifting out trash from the basin. Everyone heeds the rangers of Denali, or at least they did during my own park service patrols back in the day before Tomato's Sherpa parents sowed and raised Tomato. While relieved to be romping up with my teammates instead of following our leader's brutal pace, taxpayers everywhere would have been impressed that Tomato, a clocked-in government servant, elected trash removal over a summit attempt.

The summit morning felt a blur, wondering how I would be able to keep up with the stallions I had roped into, skeptical that I would make the top. We repeatedly passed slower climbers who warbled out oxygen-deprived versions of "Happy Birthday" to me, the frosted graybeard. Apparently, the whole roof of the continent had been let in on my secret.

Traversing above Denali Pass, I stared across Harper Basin, under the clouds, a mile away to the seldom-climbed North Peak. Like most Denali veterans, I had not climbed this eight-hundred-foot lower, yet coveted, twin peak. And I never would.

While the route up the North Peak from the west buttress off 18,200-foot Denali Pass is a moderate scramble through snowfields and bands of broken black shale, the route taken by the Sourdoughs, on the opposite side of the peak, is difficult and complex. In places, the Pioneer Ridge is no broader than a kitchen table. In the understated patois of mountaineering, it would be an "interesting climb" under a sturdy wind or while dealing with the dizzying effects of high altitude. Today, oxygen-deprived climbers monitor one another by performing the drunk driver test, walking heel to toe—stumble and you have no business getting any higher. But they didn't know this in 1910.

After supposedly summiting the North Peak, the Sourdoughs turned back around to make their unroped return down the Pioneer Ridge, which would have proved a nerve-wracking trapeze act–descent. While the southeast side merely plummets several thousand feet over steep cliffs to the Harper Glacier, the northwest side plunges an attention-grabbing thirteen thousand feet down the Wickersham Wall to the Peters Glacier: the largest vertical rise of any escarpment on the surface of the planet.

After the Sourdoughs descended a thousand feet while carefully stomping in their creepers (a flimsy, less-spiked version of the modern crampon), they reached the Sourdough Couloir, topped by a several-hundred-yard-wide, icy fan, peppered with broken rock that would slide away if you stepped on it. The gully then tapers down into a pink-granite- and black-shale-sided chute of mixed snow and ice, often echoing with rockfall, until hitting the Harper Glacier 1,900 feet later. Unrepeated (as everyone reminds you) since 1910. Thanks to their speed up and down this chute, the crevassed glacier and the steep ridges, these neophyte climbers remain the predominant legend, or myth, of Denali.

The time had come, I figured—trying to distract myself from the two thousand feet still to be suffered up to the summit—for someone to debunk the unbelievable Sourdoughs. As I crested the last steep and awkwardly angled ice to the pass, I whacked my ax in for every other slanting step. While watching Sergeant Hamilton's tentative moves in front of me, I wondered why at least one of the 1910 unroped climbers didn't fall off the steep North Peak route, particularly during the tricky descent. How did these beginners survive while the experienced Czech skier didn't? He had all the modern tools and techniques yet still bought the farm as Denali's 122nd victim. Climbing falls caused most of these deaths. Inevitably, more would soon follow.

Provided that we made it back down the mountain safely, provided I summited, this day would be the best birthday gift I could force myself into, but I had to figure out whether my pioneer heroes had topped out too. Their climb had been a mystery long enough. *Would I have even climbed Denali*, I wondered, *without legends like the Sourdoughs to inspire me?*

We finished slugging from our water bottles, peeing, and squeezing Goo into our mouths. I suggested that Inman take a Diamox tablet for his headache, caused by a traumatic brain injury earned in combat and aggravated by high altitude. I thought of both Jeff Hamilton and Cory Inman as selfless models for service to our country, and while I would do most anything to see them make the summit, they probably wouldn't need my help. Then we pulled on our packs and headed slowly, ever so slowly, up into clouds. *No way we're going to make the top*, I thought. *And if this weather turns, we're screwed.*

PART I

April 1910

High above their diggings in the mining district of Kantishna, three Alaskan prospectors stopped to catch their breath in the thin, subzero air of America's highest peak. They had launched the most outrageous and difficult ascent in the early annals of mountaineering.

They knew that their leader, Tom Lloyd, had boasted up a storm back in Fairbanks that got them here. But while worried about how his storytelling might cloud their achievement, there was no stopping now. They'd spent the whole winter preparing. They were going up.

Lloyd, Peter Anderson, William Robert Taylor, and Charles McGonagall were already renowned among the tight fraternity of northerners for pioneering winter trails and deep-shafted mines. According to Lloyd's in-depth story released two months later in the *New York Times*, they had spent the gray, dawn hours of April 3, 1910, weaving up a difficult ridge. This white, wind-blasted spine—later named Karstens Ridge—yawned from 11,000 to 14,600 feet and had already cost them several days of preparatory shoveling.

In the early twentieth century, most alpinists slogged up low-angled peaks tied to their guides with hemp ropes, lugging scientific equipment, clad in tweedy sport coats, and clutching ice axes with four-point, "creeper" claws strapped to their leather boots for traction. No one carried shovels. The old-school purists hammered in small spikes, called hobnails, through their boot soles. But on Denali, the four neophytes were unknowingly redefining alpinism. They disdained ropes, didn't understand their barometer (which they lost), wore striped cotton parkas made out of mattress ticking, wielded awkward eight-foot-long pike poles instead of axes and were shod with innovative nine-point galvanized sheet-metal crampon-creepers under knee-high moccasins made of moose hide. As if the steep terrain wasn't challenge enough, they hefted a fourteen-foot, twenty-five-pound flagpole—cut out of the forest below—over their shoulders. Along with their medieval pike poles, they charged up the mountain like errant knights ready to lance their enemy.

They had come to Alaska to seek their fortunes and make their own rules, to escape the factory lands, to live free in the fresh air. Government be damned. So it followed, logically, that even here on the isolated mountain, they were ignoring the conventions of turn-of-the-century alpinism by climbing so lightly clad with cumbersome pike poles, moving hastily across such unjustifiably dangerous and unknown terrain. No one had ever committed to a route of this scale or steepness.

They were climbing unroped, an amazing act of bravado given so much space beneath their feet. A single misplaced step on the steep, snow-blanketed east side of the ridge would've sent them into bouncing arcs more than a mile down to the Tralieka Glacier. The ridge itself stretched several times higher than the world's tallest skyscraper, Madison Avenue's Met Life Tower; the ridge proffered no rock, soil, or bare earth to step upon. Its only two flat, small resting spots were covered with an ever-shifting mantle of snow. The more forgiving north slope of the ridge, although not initially as steep, eventually dropped off into a sheer, unstable formation soon to be named the Harper Icefall. It resembled an enormous frozen waterfall, breaking the otherwise smooth-surfaced glacier into an ice cliff that periodically cascaded refrigerator-to-boxcar-sized ice blocks into the valley below. This hanging glacier—compressed from ancient snowflakes into cerulean-white, gem hardness—was one of many encircling and guarding the upper half of the mountain. (Over the next century, dozens of climbers would become irretrievably crushed and buried when these hanging glaciers exploded.)

Below this disconcerting real estate, the miners could just make out their "Tunnel Camp" at the head of the ice valley that they renamed "Wall Street." Already named eight years earlier for a government surveyor (a name that the contrary prospectors ignored), the Muldrow Glacier is riddled with deep, hidden crevasses. This sluggish, thirty-four-mile-long, frozen river of ice groaned and cracked and bulldozed against its shoreline of towering peaks. It had done so, they knew, since long before humankind had seen the mountain. Their Wall Street curled out of sight into a jumbled black terminus of precariously perched argillite boulders and other worthless rock till feeding the McKinley River.

Not adverse to risks as knowledgeable miners and Alaskan pioneers, these men had never climbed a mountain before. But they were on a mission that had nothing to do with gold. As the story goes, they would top out on this heretofore unknown ridge, then verge off onto even steeper terrain to the summit and back, all in one day. More than eight thousand feet, round-trip, at high altitude and in winter conditions. Up and down a steep, hard ice gully and snow ridge without ropes or knowledge of climbing techniques.

Today's experts who have repeatedly climbed the mountain and have examined the route describe the 1910 accomplishment as unbelievable partly because the climb has never been repeated. There are modern, professional alpinists capable of climbing the route without ropes. They would benefit, of course, from route descriptions, maps, and photographs showing each rugosity on the mountain. But these athletes would not attempt to match the first ascensionists' speed in winter with such primitive gear and a heavy flagpole over their shoulders.

While these 1910 miners and their backgrounds are forgotten, contemporary historians call them simply (yet erroneously) "the Sourdoughs." Much of their climb remains misunderstood and shrouded in mystery. But now—aided by new research and modern technology—the veracity of their ascent and how they actually performed it can be teased out, explained, and, ultimately, revealed.

To understand their story, it's helpful to look to what little is known about their lives. Lest they be forgotten.

The porcine Welshman, Lloyd, had a gift, as a mining entrepreneur, for discovering underground minerals and countless aboveground opportunities. He would make and lose a fortune in gold. As the Carbon County sheriff in Utah, he repeatedly shot it out with wanted murderers. Once he even led a posse that tracked down the infamous outlaw Butch Cassidy to his hideout in the southern part of that state.

His employee, McGonagall, was a lifelong, irritable bachelor and jack of all trades whose name was spelled at least four different ways but still ended up on the map denoting his discovery of the crucial access pass (seldom used by modern climbers) to the mountain. Like all three of his partners, Denali was the only mountain in his life.

The handsome Swede, Anderson, would outlive his first two wives and later, as a septuagenarian, marry a woman twenty-three years younger. At forty-three, his employer, Lloyd, called him "indefatigable" on the mountain, and, apparently, everywhere else.

Taylor, Lloyd's Canadian partner, was a slab of muscle, friendly and hardworking, while his 1937 interview—given on the fly as he emerged from a wilderness dogsled trip at a Denali roadhouse—filled in some of the blanks about their misunderstood climb.

Pulling together the obscure pieces, their climb would be widely praised. Bill Sherwonit, author of *To the Top of Denali*, asked a score of veteran Alaskan climbers in the 1980s to name the most significant ascents in the state and learned that the 1910 climb resonated more than any other achievement. One respondent, a former mountain guide, called the Sourdoughs "superhuman by today's standards."

Their supposed accomplishment also remains more than an unforgettable Alaskan ascent. "Eventually," wrote the historian Dee Molenaar in the 2002 *American Alpine Journal* (the worldwide almanac of climbing), "it was deemed one of the greatest feats in mountaineering history."

It was also widely accepted that no one had ever climbed so high before 1910, despite several attempts. Aside from the climbing challenge, the journey demanded route-finding, bushwhacking, boating, hunting, and dogsledding skills just to reach the mountain's base. Crudely surveyed at twenty thousand feet a dozen years earlier, Denali itself remained unmapped terra incognita.

These particular four miners called the peak "Mac" after the assassinated President McKinley, but it would take another seven years for Congress to officially switch the age-old Denali name to Mt. McKinley. As three penurious gold prospectors, and Lloyd a conservative party activist, the 1910 climbers cherished their departed Republican, William McKinley. Although he never visited Alaska, he signed the Gold Standard Act that backed American currency and further elevated the value of the precious yellow metal.

The miners had undertaken this audacious climb from the north, because the outsider Dr. Cook, a Democrat, claimed to summit from the inaccessible south side during the snowy month of September 1906. This boast incensed most Alaskans, fanned into rage, in part, by the Fairbanks newspaper editor W.F. Thompson, who referred to Cook and other easterners clambering onto their mountain as "bespectacled highbrows." Only sturdy men of the North, whipped into shape by laboring in the wilderness and living on the frozen trail, had what it took to climb *To the Top of the Continent*—the title of Cook's 1908 book. Since the climb was widely believed to be a fairy tale, someone needed to summit if only to prove Cook hadn't deposited a flag or anything else up there. And only an Alaskan could do it.

Alaskans who paid penance year round in the mosquito-rich, frost-feathered wilds—lugging fermented pouches of sourdough under their shirts to prevent the bread and donut "starter" from freezing—were called Sourdoughs. Or so the modern legend goes.

The mountain of confusion that surrounds their 1910 climb begins with the word sourdough. As an ancient bread dough recipe, French bakers introduced it in the States by bringing it to San Francisco during the 1849 gold rush. The word then became famous in America as the honorific for

California gold prospectors, who carried the dough out in the wilderness. Unlike normal yeast bread, and characterizing the hardy miners who depended upon it, the fermented and tangy dough "starter" created by the growth of bacteria kept for long periods without spoiling. Refrigerating (rather than freezing) the starter outside a tent at night slows the growth of bacteria; keeping it warm and adding flour and water increases the bacterial growth and sour taste. Even after baking, the lactic acid in the bread keeps it from spoiling without refrigeration, making it the ideal trail food.

A half century later, gold prospectors—including Lloyd, Taylor, Anderson, and McGonagall—rushing to the Canadian Klondike would have also, theoretically, earned the epithet, while snugging the dough into insulated belts and undershirt pouches to keep it warm during subzero winters. Robert Service's 1907 best-selling book *Songs of a Sourdough* helped rename the northern prospectors. Their new appellation stuck like gluey bread dough, and then rose in popularity— but mostly with the uninitiated who lived outside of Alaska. While new residents throughout the North aspired to being respected and accepted by the more experienced frontiersmen, being elevated to some sort of Sourdough status after surviving the gauntlet of winter and living in Alaska for a full year became a cliché and a catchy myth created by imaginative outsiders. After World War II, lower forty-eight residents flocked north, expanding the population, bringing the mythical name into common use as if it had always been part of the Alaskan lexicon.

The truth is that back in the day, the four miners on Denali—along with the Alaskan newspapers reporting on them—called themselves "pioneers." This title also referred to the Pioneers of Alaska, a statewide organization started in 1904, requiring only that its members be white men who had lived for at least one year in Alaska.

Since the hypothetical Denali conqueror Dr. Cook chose to live outside the land of these pioneers, leaving him unqualified for induction, the leathery denizens of the North reckoned him a dandy and a "Cheechako," which was a popular description throughout Alaska and the United States. This word, like Sourdough, also originated outside Alaska, from the Seattle area, where Chinook Indians combined "chee" and "chako" for "newcomer." Still, the pioneers of the north, along with three other Cheechako expeditions to Denali, all wanted to prove Cook a fraud.

If not for this newcomer Cook inspiring this frenzied race to summit Denali, it might have taken decades for the mountain to be climbed. So as a rival of the Sourdough pioneers, his tortured yet well-documented days provide more than a few clues into who really climbed the mountain and how they did it. Cook's life opens a window into understanding the mountain's history, its pull on climbers and the inscrutable Sourdoughs.

⁓

Dr. Frederick A. Cook launched his first attempt in June 1903 from sea level, at the Dena'ina Athapaskan village of Tyonek, Alaska. Off to a shaky start, Cook's team nearly lost fifteen packhorses in the dangerous tide—lacking boat ramps they threw the horses overboard and let them swim ashore in ice water. He and his five companions then split apart to drive their packhorses toward the Alaska Range, while they watched the Mt. Redoubt volcano belch flames to the south.

Much can be learned about Cook through his books and even more tomes written about him. If he were alive today, muttering to himself while oblivious to his companions, he would quickly be diagnosed with the classic symptoms of Asperger's syndrome: impaired social interactions, repetitive project obsessions, intense focus on oneself, and speech impairments or trouble vocalizing. To wit, Cook mixed awkwardly with others, he became obsessed with exploration and ethnology, he was a loner, and he had a lisp. One of his companions described his drooping moustache and the blank look on his face. He looked like he was trying to connect the untethered dots in his head.

Also characteristic of Asperger's, Cook was an expressive writer. In *To the Top of the Continent*, he wrote about their quest: "This peak like a star on a cloudy night would blink and disappear with marvelous quickness. It did not seem to us as being very far away, nor did it give the impression of great altitude, but there was a mystery about the thing which kept one's attention pointed."

With exacting self-orientation, he abstained from the accepted expedition narrative form by failing to introduce his five teammates. Instead, he commented that he made no mistake in their selection. Oddly, he refers to the "faithfulness" of his men, but by the time he penned those words his journalist teammate Robert Dunn had flagrantly and publicly betrayed his leadership in print.

Cook's Montana horse packer, Fred Printz, had beaten a trail out of Tyonek the year before while employed by the US Geological Surveyor, Alfred H. Brooks. During Cook's journey, he regularly referred to Brooks's "Plans for Climbing

Mt. McKinley" article from that January's *National Geographic Magazine*.

They spent a month hacking through what Cook called "the jungle," fording glacial rivers up toward the southern crest of the six-hundred-mile-long Alaska Range. The trek thus far was ambitious, at times even desperate, but not innovative—thanks to the pioneering of Brooks (responsible for naming the Muldrow Glacier after a colleague).

Cook described how "circles of alders and willows and small lakes covered with pond lilies made the park-like picture complete." To northern pioneers, this whitewashed scene implied bushwhacking with wet feet through god-awful clouds of mosquitoes.

But the Cheechako government man Brooks, whom pioneers actually admired for his long journeys, told it like it was. "Five years of Alaska travel," Brooks wrote, "have convinced me that there is no hardship so difficult to bear as this insect pest.... Men capable of enduring heat and cold, hunger and fatigue without murmuring, will become almost savage under the torture."

By early August, the mosquitoes disappeared as Cook crossed the Alaska Range and turned northeast across the cooler, northern tundra. They were trailed by wolves and foxes, and with plentiful fresh game and rifle ammunition, they ate moose, caribou, and grizzly bear meat. After blundering up the wrong glacial valley, they retraced their steps and then turned back south onto the dirty ice of the Peters Glacier. This ice highway ran directly beneath the north side of Mt. McKinley, parallel to the Muldrow Glacier and separated by the saw-toothed, eleven-mile-long Pioneer Ridge. Cook wrote that to this point, they had covered 500 miles (Dunn called it 450; today's maps show less than 250 miles to this point).

Cook often remained silent when his men awaited direction, and given his drive to climb the mountain, he seemed indecisive, even impulsive: the original space cadet. Characteristically, he had a skewed sense of direction and couldn't help getting lost.

While the Alaska press savaged Cook in general for being an outsider, his tell-all teammate, Dunn, got down and dirty with specific character assassination. In a series of *Outing Magazine* articles later enlarged into his book *The Shameless Diary of An Explorer*, Dunn called Cook "the professor," which spoke to the airs of the expedition leader, because Dunn, as a recent Harvard graduate, would hardly see himself as the student of a doctor graduated from a non-ivy league institution. Dunn, amid many put-downs, described Cook's attempt to route-find with a pencil and a straw on their primitive map, instead of using their small surveying telescope: "'There's a good chance to use your theodolite now,' said [their photographer Walter] Miller today, pointing to an angle of Muldrow [Glacier], whose direction of flow we had been arguing about. The professor only smiled, and never touched an instrument— as often before when we've wanted an observation."

They left their dwindling horse population (they'd lost two) untethered and grazing on the grassy slopes near the glacier's toe. Then the five men tied themselves together with horsehair ropes and spent two days circling or jumping over crevasses as they traveled up Peters Glacier. Finally, they climbed a low-angled icefall up to the fern line, where permanent snow flimsily bridged even more crevasses, hidden like human flytraps.

Denali's north face towered over their heads, bigger than any wall they would see in their lives. Mouths agape, they watched wet snow avalanches billow up into clouds that Cook called "vapours," flowing and roaring down toward them, hitting the cracked-apart glacier floor—and shaking it, Cook said, like an earthquake—congealing faster than cement in chaotic, rock-sprinkled sundaes of debris. They gave these cataclysms wide berth by hugging the western edge of the glacier.

Their loaded canvas rucksacks weighed forty pounds and contained ingeniously light, three-pound silk tents, down robe jackets that doubled as sleeping bags, gas stoves, and a simple kitchen, with one kettle for melting snow. They subsisted on twenty-pound cans of pemmican (fatty meat mixed with fruit), biscuits, sourdough bread they had baked several days earlier, cheese gone bad, condensed milk, and tea.

Led by the burly, step-chopping arm of Printz, using the latest ice axes, Dunn wrote, "It seemed to take ten minutes to cut each step" up the initial, forty-degree slope of the Northwest Buttress—one rocky spoke of a dozen more ridges that wheeled around Denali's twin peaks. Since Dunn lacked an ice ax, he used a willow tent pole as a cane.

Their route rimmed the cacophonous, unstable north face. While thankful that their steepening granite buttress would shed all the big avalanches, they followed the hardened, cement-like snow from an old and small avalanche track up the buttress in order to avoid breaking trail through deep snow. They camped at ten thousand feet.

Mountaineers had not yet figured out the optimal time of year to attempt Denali. Local miners only knew that late summer held unsettled, wet weather.

Still, Cook had already outperformed a party of Alaskan climbers who reached 8,100 feet on the Peters Glacier that June. They took one look at the world-class north wall (later named the Wickersham Wall) and beat a hasty retreat. Their leader, Judge Wickersham, "reluctantly concluded" in his diary that "there is no possible chance of further ascent from this side of Denali at this season—or any other season for that matter." He made the most of his long journey, staking out a prospect in a Kantishna creek and stimulating a gold rush by advertising the region's mineral potential in the *Fairbanks Daily News Miner*, a newspaper he'd created to finance the expedition that would later become instrumental in promoting the Sourdough climb.

As for the scantily sponsored Cook, climbing even this far on a steepening buttress showed incredible cheekiness, if not naiveté. His ambitions, Dunn believed, easily outweighed his climbing experience.

On August 30, "checkmated" when the granite cliffs became too steep for mere scrambling, they made their final camp at eleven thousand feet. It was the same elevation, halfway around the mountain, where the Sourdoughs would establish their last camp and begin their day-long sprint to the top in 1910.

"It ain't that we can't find a way that's possible, taking chances," Printz said. "There ain't no way!" (It took a half century and one of North America's finest climbers, Fred Beckey, to hammer pitons into the granite walls and finish the technical route.)

They quickly descended back into Peter's Basin. After walking what Cook called twenty-nine miles (less than half that distance, according to the modern map) back to the glacier toe, Dunn and the others searched for horses while the professor "lazed in camp." Two days later, they rounded up only seven of their horses. If bears and wolves had not already eaten the other six, they were likely being stalked as Cook sat in stony silence, contemplating his next move.

Aware of the Denali creation story, Dunn wrote about a raven circling above, like Chief Totson, squawking at the hungry climbers below: "Can't get out of this country before winter. You're fools, but we like human carrion. We've got you. Ha!"

Finally, after a council of war, cut off from retreating south because the grass for horses would be frozen, they decided to make a desperate dash east across unmapped country. They pinned all their hopes on discovering a new pass that would take them south over the Alaska Range.

By this time Dunn had reached his limits with their leader. "I think he would face death and disaster without a word," Dunn wrote, "but through the insensitiveness of age and too much experience, rather than by true courage. I cannot believe he has imagination; of a leader's qualities has not shown one. He seems our sympathetic servant."

⚊⚊

While Dunn knew of his leader's prior polar experiences, he had little sympathy for the hardships that had shaped the enigmatic, thirty-eight-year-old doctor. At only four years old, "Freddy" lost his father to illness, then a sister. He grew up as the youngest of three siblings in Brooklyn, New York. To support his mother he worked through public school as an office boy, a rent collector, and with his distinguishing ambition, opened a printing business. He later wrote in his book *Return From the North Pole* of his "innate and abnormal desire for exploration" so that he might make "some extraordinary accomplishment."

Following in the footsteps of his physician father, he paid his way through medical school by starting a milk-delivery business with a brother. In 1889, he married a stenographer, Libby Forbes. A year later, amid Cook's final exams at the College of Physicians and Surgeons, his wife gave birth to a baby who died within hours. As peritonitis set in, Libby lived only another week. Dr. Cook, twenty-five, tried to lose himself in his new profession but found few patients. He staved off late-hour loneliness and melancholy by reading innumerable exploration accounts.

Not unlike the prospectors who fled north, Cook had had enough of "the life sapping conditions of modern city life," he wrote, with its "hothouse, germ-cultivated air, [where] the muscles wither from disease." In 1891, the year after Libby died, he signed on as the surgeon for Robert Peary's reconnaissance of Greenland, to determine whether it were an island or a peninsula. Peary was a narcissistic Navy lieutenant, driven to become first to reach the North Pole. By expedition's end, he spoke highly of Cook, who exhibited great patience, in addition to his skills as an ethnologist, studying the local Inuit. Also as a doctor, he saved the day by expertly splinting Peary's leg, broken in two places as their ship rammed through the ice pack. (Ten years later, Cook returned to the Arctic and rescued Peary, suffering from scurvy and heart issues.)

Within a year of docking back in Brooklyn, Cook signed on again as a ship surgeon, this time on the Belgian Antarctic Expedition's *RV Belgica*. In the interest of making history to become the first to winter over on the southernmost continent, the captain imprudently jammed *Belgica* into the Bellingshausen Sea pack ice in February 1898. Then, as total darkness descended and the ship's leader banned eating the disagreeable-tasting penguin and seal meat, many of the crew became ill. Morale plummeted. Several of the crew lost their mind. One abandoned the ship and set off across the sea ice, planning to walk back home, never to be seen again.

When the captain and the ship's leader fell ill, confined to their berths and writing their wills, Dr. Cook calmly diagnosed scurvy. He and the first mate, the Norwegian explorer Roald Amundsen, then took command of the ship. Although vitamin C had not yet been discovered as a cure for scurvy, Cook's experience in the Arctic had shown him that fresh meat would prevent the disease, so he put penguin and seal back on the galley table and prescribed it as everyone's daily medicine. Within months, the entire crew recovered.

Still trapped in ice seven feet thick, fearing that they would have to try to survive another mind-blowing winter trapped in the pack, Cook suggested cutting trenches a half mile to open water. After a month's digging and dynamiting, towing the ship, the *Belgica* finally floated free. They had been imprisoned in ice for thirteen months. Cook had regularly and cheerfully treated crew members for various ailments, arguably saving a number of lives through his coolheaded management. Amundsen called him the most popular man on the ship. Although technically a Cheechako with no climbing experience, his leadership skills in subzero survival situations—no worse than that of the 1910 Sourdoughs— left him mostly qualified to tackle North America's highest, coldest mountain. As for Cook's eccentricities and social skills on board, his position as the respected physician, along with the language barrier between him and most of his Belgian shipmates, allowed him to get away with his weirdly aloof behavior.

The first duplicity of his expedition career would begin on his way home. Whether it was ambition, the drive for fame, or anger at the blows dealt out to him by the cruel fates, Cook's honorable and compassionate qualities began to shift in order that he fulfill his imagined destiny as explorer and ethnologist. In Tierra del Fuego, ever the smooth operator, he convinced the Anglican missionary Thomas Bridges to loan out his life's work: a thirty-thousand-word Yahgan language dictionary on the indigenous people of southern Argentina. Cook promised that he would help publish the work, then return the manuscript.

By mid-September 1903, strung out on their daring Denali circumnavigation, Cook's team had discovered a pass. Pulling and pushing the exhausted horses across a glacier, they left winter on the treeless north side and crossed over the Alaska Range down into the headwaters of the Bull River. Several days later, no longer able to beat through the thickening south-side jungle, they built a raft alongside on the flooding Chulitna River.

But the horses wouldn't fit on the tiny raft. "Each man had among the animals one or two pets," Cook wrote, "and no one had the boldness to deliberately kill any of the noble creatures." They abandoned them to what both Cook and Dunn described in their books as certain death, but Dunn alone described how Cook had no interest in the animals.

Five years after the event, Cook wrote in his book that all the horses had made it through two winters. Given prolific predators, along with the remote, subzero conditions of the region, it wouldn't have taken a sharp reader to wonder whether Cook was telling the truth.

At this point, his three-month circumnavigation of the Denali massif proved his best exploratory accomplishment, even if he had not attempted one of the mountain's more difficult routes. Cook had found the same path to fame that obsessed Peary.

Still, Cook had lacked his former leader's considerable sponsorship. So he had charged his teammates $1,000 each. Dunn got the money from a well-to-do aunt and claimed he gave it up to Cook early, mainly to prevent Cook's exceedingly buxom, wealthy wife from joining the expedition and causing distractive chaos among the men. In gratitude for the contribution, Dunn bestowed his Aunt Hunter's name on a twelve-thousand-foot-plus domed peak that they saw from their Denali high camp (mapmakers mistakenly gave the name to the steep, 14,573-foot mountain Dunn could not see). Cook's well-to-do wife, eager to please her darling Fred, paid for everything else.

Before he had even left Alaska, he was plotting his return, cabling the press, angling for the notoriety and fame that would in turn bring sponsorship. Planting a flag atop McKinley would merely allow him to find backers to finance his North Pole obsession.

———

Three years after his circumnavigation, financed by a magazine advance and a promised $10,000 contribution (worth $249,000 in 2018) from a wealthy big-game hunter, Cook returned to Tyonek, Alaska, in June 1906. This time he had surrounded himself with more experienced alpinists: Hershel Parker, a cerebral mining engineer and Columbia University professor, would colead the expedition. He in turn invited friends: the topographer Russell Porter and Belmore Browne. A muscular hunter and powerful climber who first visited Alaska at eight years old, Browne had studied at the New York School of Art and the Académie Julian in Paris (his wildlife paintings and mountain dioramas still hang in museums from Washington, DC, to Anchorage). Browne proved to be a charismatic and popular member of any outing he joined. Parker and he—already inseparable adventure pals—would come to know the mountain and its approaches more intimately than any men of their time.

But this year, Cook, a reluctant pathfinder at best, made a major tactical error. Instead of circling around to the eastern pass that he had found three years earlier, they tried to shortcut through the dense alder forests with a power-boat directly from the south. Once off the boat, they wasted good climbing weather in thankless labor, plodding through mosquito bogs trying to reach the mountain's remote base. Finally, they penetrated far enough up onto a lower glacier to see, that from the southeast side, as Browne said, "the mountain looked absolutely unclimbable." Just as most horse-pack train disdaining Alaskans had always known. Of Cook's two dozen packhorses—burned up in a coal seam fire, lost in rivers, or too weak to travel—none survived the trip.

Depleted physically, with winter snapping at their heels, they were defeated. Even worse, their wealthy patron reneged on both the hunt and the promised financing, and since Cook was being sued for losing the horses, he plunged into debt. At this pivotal moment, according to his biographers, he couldn't help but thinking that a victory on the mountain would provide financial salvation.

Denied his dreams, stripped of his finances, Cook decided to force matters, for once, into a successful outcome. First, he got rid of all the real climbers in his party. He sent Browne, Miller, and Printz across the state to collect animal specimens; Parker returned to New York. Cook announced that he and Barrill would merely explore another river approach to Denali.

Several weeks later, Browne returned to the coast and heard the rumor that Cook and Barrill had climbed the mountain. He was stunned. There hadn't been time for Cook to do more than a reconnoiter.

When they met up again, Cook, to Browne's surprise, confirmed the rumor. So he took his good friend Barrill aside; he told Browne: "I can tell you all about the big peaks just south of the mountain, but if you want to know about Mount McKinley, go and ask Cook." But Browne, along with Parker, at least for a short time, supported Cook even if they held private doubts. Like other skeptics they waited to see Cook's proof.

His hastily written book *To the Top of the Continent* came out in 1908. Cook wrote that he and Barrill shouldered light, forty-five-pound packs with only ten days' food and the same gear they'd used on the Northwest Buttress. He carried a three-by-five-inch camera, and thanks to his and Miller's skills as lensmen during both McKinley trips, the book was handsomely illustrated. In the florid writing style (later deigned as purple prose) of the day, Cook described his final approach to the mountain in great detail.

Prospectors in Kantishna—living under the northern shadow of the great mountain, passing around the book in the mining camps with fascination—could pinpoint where the well-described details in Cook's approach story switched to that of a vague fairy tale. The fanciful writing style began right when Cook and Barrill left the low-angled glacier.

Amazingly, Cook described circling around from the southern Ruth Glacier (named after his daughter) and up steep, avalanche-prone technical terrain to a difficult ridge. Building snow houses or tying themselves into ice axes while bivouacked on sixty-degree ice slopes, they approached the last slope to the summit after less than a week's climb.

"We edged up along a steep snowy ridge and over the heaven-scraped granite to the top," Cook wrote, "AT LAST! The soul-stirring task was crowned with victory; the top of the continent was under our feet." Cook photographed Barrill on a summit with a flag suspended off an ice ax.

This black-and-white photograph showed the lightly clad Barrill holding a flag out from his waist in the middle distance. They carried no hooded parkas and had lost their creepers a month earlier (of the tens of thousands of successful Denali summiteers in the last century, no one has climbed without creepers or crampons—on his 1903 attempt, Cook constantly slipped and slid without them). Still, to most of Cook's lay readership, a summit photograph captioned "To the top of the Continent" would serve as proof.

Summit photographs, as much as a lone teammate's corroboration or journals or barometric measurements, are the most expedient way for a mountaineer to enter the record books. Ever since cameras were invented—at the same time technical mountaineering began—a clean and identifiable summit photograph acts as both judge and jury. So Cook took great trouble to obtain one.

As for the descent, the neophyte climber Cook then used a single sentence to describe a "less-difficult," four-day "tumble-down" return to the glacier, with no mention of the challenge of down-climbing or rappelling (Cook and Barrill lacked the gear and knowledge to descend by sliding down their ropes). For Browne, who had witnessed Cook clumsily falling and getting trapped on a low-angle snowfield earlier that summer, the descent seemed even more improbable than the climb. Cook had somehow managed to descend difficult technical terrain as if it were child's play.

They had spent less than two weeks, approaching, climbing, and descending an utterly unknown route on North America's highest mountain. Although the cowboy Barrill had previously ridden or chased horses over hill and dale, neither man had climbed a major, glaciated peak in their lives.

Few Alaskans believed Cook. But his sponsors did, if only on the strength of Cook's perceived character, even before his *Continent* hit the bookstores. To those who didn't climb mountains or sledge to the poles, Cook's descriptions of his epic journeys seemed plenty believable. After all, he was a respected physician, he accompanied and later rescued Peary in the Arctic, he saved lives in Antarctica, and he had already explored the Denali massif—why would he lie about climbing it? Cook's reputation was also burnished by his May 1907 *Harper's Magazine* article about the climb, showing a cropped version of the infamous summit photograph.

In the meantime, debtors hounded him, he had drained his wife's coffers and he couldn't pay his horse packer Printz's wages. By July 1907, Cook turned in the manuscript for his

McKinley book and quietly sailed out of Massachusetts for northern Greenland. This time he'd been funded in advance by another wealthy big-game hunter who accompanied Cook north.

Throughout 1908, in Cook's absence, it wasn't enough for him to have claimed the top of the continent or to have published stories about it to set the Sourdoughs in motion up Denali. For the time being, while thousands of "boomers" had abandoned Kantishna in 1906, Lloyd, Taylor, McGonagall, and Anderson were among less than a hundred who remained, prying, tunneling, and toiling upon mostly worthless prospects that took all of their time and energy. The mountain would have to wait.

Seemingly oblivious to what the world thought of him, in the throes of his final obsession, Dr. Cook now chased hard after his destiny, a word he would use repetitively in his book about the North Pole, but not once in *To the Top of the Continent*. If he could reach the North Pole, it would atone for his financial woes and distract his detractors, allowing him to escape further questions about his incredible Denali ascent.

In April 1909, Cook emerged from his second winter on ice to announce that he had become the first man to reach the North Pole—fulfilling, it would seem, his destiny. President Taft wired congratulations.

The details of what Cook claimed to do and how he did it mattered little to Alaskans. These pioneers only knew that, regardless of the international clamor Cook had stirred up, he had wrongly robbed a piece of the mother lode from their own backyard. The pioneers were also paying more attention now because their promising prospects in Kantishna had come to naught.

For the time being, Alaskans read in the papers that Cook had bested Peary, who claimed to reach the northernmost point of the planet a year later. The controversy burned into a white heat. Newspaper polls from Toronto to Pittsburgh overwhelmingly believed Cook over Peary.

Everything changed that fall, when the *New York Times* published an affidavit, signed by the handlebar-mustached cowboy Barrill, that he and Cook had climbed a small mountain, not exceeding 6,000 feet, which was more than a dozen miles away from Mt. McKinley (more than 14,000 feet above). Barrill also swore that he wrote false data in his diary under the dictation of Dr. Cook. Nor did it hurt Barrill's case that Peary's supporters had paid him today's equivalent of over $100,000 to sign the affidavit.

The consensus began to shift. If Cook lied about McKinley, the thinking went, why wouldn't he lie about the North Pole? Since his log books had been "lost," he wouldn't or couldn't share his navigational data for the Arctic trip, and those who had read Dunn's *Shameless Diary* learned that Cook couldn't route-find on dry land, never mind across shifting sea ice to the pole. The 1909 Cook–Peary controversy spewed as much ink as any other adventure story in the new century.

Even the Alaskan newspapers weighed in: "Ever since Dr. Cook described his ascent of Mount McKinley," the *Fairbanks Times* explained about the pole debate, "Alaskans have been suspicious of the accuracy of this explorer."

By this time, tasked by the Explorers Club to follow Cook's route, his 1906 teammates Parker and Browne began planning their own return to Denali. The race was on. But the Sourdoughs would beat them to the punch.

Thomas Lloyd recalled that his McKinley climb started in November 1909. The most popular version of their legend is that it began with a bet. Still, no gambler ever publicly claimed any winnings. Depending on the storyteller, the wager varied from two cents to $5,000—shouted out as a joke to Lloyd on the streets of town among a large crowd.

It is fact, like many other famous expeditions, that everything started in a bar, called the Washington, or (Bill) McPhee's Saloon. Lloyd had been drinking with the owner Bill, whom he'd met at McPhee's first saloon in Dawson City during the Klondike gold rush. When the Klondike went bust, all the Dawson bordellos, banks, stores, and bars—keeping their signage—moved 250 miles due west, to open up Fairbanks, known as the American Klondike.

McPhee's Saloon, on the dirt corner of Lacy and First Streets, had a reputation for its clean glasses, cold beer, and outsize personality. The watering hole would become famous for the bartender's pet moose, which developed a fondness for chasing down potatoes and stale bread with alcohol—causing no end of havoc as the moose got drunk. Since the mayor's repeated demands to remove the moose from the Saloon were refused, he drew up a town ordinance prohibiting moose on the city sidewalks—so that the large ungulate couldn't lawfully enter the bar. So the patrons killed the moose and ate it. (Years later, as the saloon got torn down, workers found $8,500 in $20 gold coins stuffed in a wall.)

That subzero day in November 1909, near the glowing woodstove, McPhee and Lloyd shared more than a few beers. "To prove whether that fellow Cook made the climb or not I will willingly give $500 myself to have the ascent made,"

McPhee said in a dialogue more suitable to a pulp fiction adventure novel than a *New York Times Magazine* exclusive.

McPhee added, according to the *Times* story, that "no living man could make the ascent."

So Lloyd boasted that he and another "fellow"—McGonagall—had been around the mountain more than had anyone else and that they could climb it.

McPhee said he was too old.

"I may be," Lloyd said, "but I can find men who will do it."

The white-haired McPhee, sixty-eight, had offered to find other sponsors to join in on what he referred to as "a game."

Within several days, Lloyd complained that one of the two Fairbanks papers made his Denali ambitions into a joke. By then, McPhee secured financial pledges from E.W. Griffin (in exchange for his six-by-twelve-foot flag being planted on top of McKinley) and Gust Peterson, a local businessman. The trio each contributed $500 (worth over $37,000 in 2018).

Lloyd and his sponsors were founding members of the Pioneers of Alaska organization. In addition to preserving member names and history, the organization's stated goal was to promote Alaska. The Fairbanks Pioneers of Alaska "Igloo," or branch, was one of five, rapidly expanding to thirty-six, throughout the north.

The *Times* article continued: "If any one, (I don't claim to be anybody,) any Easterner can make that climb, us pioneers can skin them," Lloyd said. "Also, I believe conditions are more favorable for the climb at this time of year than they were when Cook claimed to have climbed it."

Lloyd brazenly planned to take advantage of winter conditions, when avalanches and crevasse bridges would be frozen over. Cook claimed to summit the mountain in September when soft conditions and frequent snowfall would've made the climb—in Alaskan's minds—impossible.

As for sponsorship, Lloyd could have raised more money, but he only wanted to cover his costs; he also needed $1,500 to finance the resupply and return trip to his Kantishna mines. So at 1 p.m. on December 22, 1909, six avenging Sourdoughs (Peter Anderson would follow later) mounted up, in a winter solstice departure offering them a scant three hours and fifty-seven minutes of daylight.

On that same day, as announced in stateside newspapers, the internationally respected scientists in Denmark made their conclusion about another sledging journey performed the previous year. "The material which has been submitted to the University for investigation," it read, referring to the navigational and journal data that Cook had finally submitted, "does not contain observations or information which could be considered to prove that Dr. Cook reached the North Pole."

While this news would effectively end Cook's explorer career, the Sourdoughs were only getting started. Cheered on by a crowd, the Sourdoughs rode out of town on sleds driven by three horses, two dog teams, and a mule. Their initial 175-mile journey to their Kantishna mining cabins in the foothills 35 miles north of Denali would take nearly a week, overnighting in whiskey-soaked roadhouse cabins on the way, their trail lit by a full moon. While colder and darker, the northern Sourdough approach proved much more comfortable than the bushwhacking, bug-swatting, river crossing ordeals that outsiders used into the southern side of the mountain. Belmore Browne, with classic Cheechako blinders to the pioneer's access, cribbed from Kipling that the mountain had "been placed 'in the most inaccessible position obtainable' . . . where 'there is no law of god nor man.'"

It took only a winter's supply of food and the prospect of finding gold to get them out to their more accessible mines. But to get them up the mountain, Lloyd had fired them up about Cook. "His boys," as Lloyd called them, also trusted him and had no clue that he'd eventually betray them or lie about their time on the mountain. Understanding Lloyd's ambitions, his charm, and how he inspired his reticent partners (whose lives remain shrouded in mystery) shows how they pulled off the most difficult climb of the new century.

Since Cook had inspired the garrulous Lloyd, it followed that he too could manufacture incredible epics out of mere hikes. He told census takers that year that he was forty-nine, but his mining partner and employees (soon to be climbing teammates) and others believed he was in his sixties.

As an atheist Welshman, Lloyd spoke in singsong, stretched-out vowels. While playing the quiet, modest, and sincere hayseed, speaking in a matter-of-fact manner, he could charm the antlers off a moose. Until "he balled it up" with stories about his climb of North America's highest alp, Lloyd proved the ideal salesman for larger-than-life Sourdough deeds right out of Robert Service's books of fictional northern poetry.

If Lloyd wasn't built for mountain climbing, he had earned his stripes as both a pioneer and a mining entrepreneur. He left Wales for Pennsylvania at eighteen, and after three years of laboring in coalfields where he had worked his way into a commissioner position, he moved to Scofield, Utah. Not wasting any time, and utilizing his instincts for promoting coal as "black gold," Lloyd found a low-grade yet lucrative seam that fueled the nearby railroad. In a few years, his mining investments and proclivity for sniffing out minerals made him a popular if not a wealthy man.

By 1892, he became the first marshal for Scofield, then the first sheriff for Utah's burgeoning Carbon County. In a territory governed by the Latter Day Saints, his meteoric rise as the first gentile lawman helped fuel a lifetime's worth of bragging. Still, his gunfights while chasing wanted murderers on horseback or while climbing box canyons were reported in many newspapers. In 1895, he married a Danish immigrant, Elizabeth Sorensen. That same year, he collected a $250 reward from the governor of Colorado for turning in a heavily armed sheriff-killing outlaw alive.

In the spring of 1896, he traded in his badge and accepted an appointment as Utah's first coalmine inspector. Lloyd collected a handsome salary and traveling expenses while assessing, reporting on, and, occasionally, investing in mineral seams around the west. The local newspapers covered his comings and goings from blackened coalmines to the Cullen, Salt Lake City's most extravagant hotel. Lloyd had become a player.

As a mining promoter, he stood up for his cronies. In the spring of 1897, troops arrested and removed a dozen of his fellow miners (half of them armed) from the Uncompahgre Indian Reservation in eastern Utah. Since the tribe objected to white men illegally prospecting for asphalt and other hydrocarbons on their land, Lloyd revisited the prospects. He told the *Salt Lake Tribune*: "Certain sentimentalists have said it was a shame to rob the redman out of what the Government had set aside for his benefit. Tell me how a man who has located a gilsonite [asphalt] claim has robbed an Indian? Why, the loafer never was known to dig for anything, and can never be taught to."

After more incautious remarks, for which he later suffered political blowback, Lloyd quickly learned how to become more guarded in front of the press. He developed a whole new soft-spoken, modest persona amid strangers. For the rest of his life—particularly after his McKinley climb—he would tiptoe around newspaper reporters.

The next month, on April 21, 1897, in Castle Gate, Utah, where Lloyd had discovered his lucrative coal seam, the notorious gunslinger Butch Cassidy boldly robbed the mine payroll in broad daylight. Inconspicuously clad in his slouch hat, milling among a crowd of miners, he pointed a six-shooter at the paymaster E.L. Carpenter's belly and took three sacks filled with over $8,000 (worth $250,000 today) of miners' pay. With a single companion, galloping out of town on saddleless racehorses and pursued by a poorly led posse, Cassidy escaped to southern Utah.

A week later, the ex-sheriff Lloyd organized a posse and spent eleven days circling Cassidy's Robber's Roost bandit hideaway in southern Utah. Most of the posse retreated after a week, but Lloyd stuck it out with the bounty hunter Pete Anderson—no relation to his climbing partner of 1910—and three others.

By now, Lloyd had accumulated many friends throughout the state. The *Tribune* concluded that he had found no one resembling the outlaws, but that he had repeatedly run into four or five tough-looking thugs and members of the Robber's

Roost gang (later referred to as "the Wild Bunch"). Lloyd told the simpatico reporter that the gang couldn't be broken up without much danger to life.

The competing *Salt Lake Herald*—knowing Cassidy's popularity and benevolent double dealings with lawmen—saw right through Lloyd. Under the subhead "They Ran Into a Double Quartette of Leading Citizens of the Roost and Lost all Desire For that $2000 Reward," the story deepened: "Lloyd swapped his cockney cap for a sombrero with one of the outlaws and Anderson swapped his worn out horse with another outlaw for a horse possessing sufficient strength to bring him home. The outlaws were as hospitable to the boys as was Paymaster Carpenter to them."

Although Lloyd naturally had an aversion to being "plugged full of hot lead" (as Butch Cassidy's partner had warned a fleeing clerk next to the paymaster, who quickly handed over a sack of silver), Lloyd didn't lack ambition. Within three months of the robbery, stricken with desire to get richer quicker in the Klondike gold fields, "Tom" resigned from his state inspector position.

Supported by three minefield investors, he left Utah, his wife, three sons, and a daughter. Boarding a train, then a steamer north out of Seattle, he and a companion built a skiff from the adjoining spruce forest to float the Yukon River. Under eight inches of new snow (as he wrote to a friend at the *Tribune*), he joined the cavalcade of hopefuls laying claim to every creek surrounding Dawson City, in the Yukon Territories of Canada. Within short order, in addition to his own staked-out prospects, he began managing one of the richest "Bonanza" lodes in the region. (Up on Denali, he would remind his teammates that he once held $400,000 in gold while working with the famed Klondike developer "Arkansas Jim" Hall.)

In 1900, for the first time in three years, he briefly returned to his family in Utah, while showing his "millionaire chief" Hall around town. Then he turned tail back to the gold fields, this time to Nome, Alaska, and then a quick fling down in San Francisco, with a woman less than half his age.

By now, the Sourdough Lloyd, much like his partners on Denali, matched the profile from Service's *Songs of a Sourdough*:

> *There's a race of men that don't fit in,*
> *A race that can't stay still;*
> *So they break the hearts of kith and kin,*
> *And they roam the world at will.*

In 1901, Thomas Lloyd, who listed his age on the certificate as forty-one, married Emelia Peterson, twenty, in San Francisco. She would briefly join him in Alaska, and then raise their newborn daughter in Seattle. No one seemed to notice that Lloyd had another wife and four children back in Utah.

In 1904, as the Nome and Klondike gold fields had gone bust and dancing stopped in the burlesques, Lloyd joined the stampede to a town recently named after McKinley's vice president, Charles Fairbanks (in hopes of gaining Territory Status for the District of Alaska). Although the gold didn't glitter as abundantly as it did in Dawson, Lloyd found this Fairbanks frontier of loose women and whiskey drinkers more to his liking than the killjoys and teetotalers in Utah. Along with being on a new American edge of undeveloped, ready-to-exploit frontier, Fairbanks—unlike the outlaw-ridden west—lacked violent gunplay. While fistfights were common, men carried firearms mostly for hunting and procuring food in Alaska. Lloyd had grown tired of being shot at in Utah.

Within three years, he became an active and founding member of the Pioneers of Alaska, the local Republican Party, and the Masonic Temple. His burning desire, of course, starting anew for the fourth time in the four decades since he had landed in America, was to become rich and famous. By most men's reckoning, he was already rich and used his grubstake to stake more mines out in Kantishna, three dozen miles away from the big mountain.

Like Cook, Tom Lloyd sought Denali for fame but only partly for money. When he put the mountain in his sights in late 1909, he had become a respectable figure in Fairbanks. No longer packing heat in a holster, he had become a political operator. He sported a walrus moustache over his jowly mien and became—as per the photograph caption of him posed with five other paunchy businessmen—one of the "Heavyweights" of Fairbanks. He was on a first name, bar-mate basis with many of the local VIPs and saloonkeepers. Fairbanks, Alaska, would become notorious as a place to escape family or government, cover one's tracks, and begin anew.

His swift Denali climb—completed under mysterious circumstances—however, would put him under a national spotlight. To understand the rest of the rambling story of the climb from the *New York Times* exclusive, it's instructive to review the preceding newspaper coverage. Having learned his lesson about talking freely to the press, he withheld the story from most everyone but his pal W.F. Thompson at the *Fairbanks News Miner*. On April 12, 1910, Thompson first broke a few details in a short piece, "Alaskans Reach Top of Summit," subheaded "Tom Lloyd and Party Reached the Summit of Mount McKinley on April 3—Claim Cook Did Not Reach the Top."

The competing *Fairbanks Daily Times* (matching the *Salt Lake Herald*'s skepticism of Lloyd) followed up with: "M'Kinley Conquered . . . is proud boast of Tom Lloyd." These cryptic, brief news pieces would be echoed, editorialized upon, or reprinted in hundreds of newspapers across the country. Meanwhile, Thompson, aligned with Lloyd's three sponsors, withheld a lengthier feature, with two dozen pictures and a detailed interview of Lloyd, for the highest bidder. He and his sponsors formed the Lloyd–Mt. McKinley Committee and promptly began fielding offers from *Colliers*, the *New York Times*, the *San Francisco Examiner*, and *Hampton's Magazine*.

Two days later, the *Seattle Star* ran its own exclusive interview and photograph of Lloyd's second wife Emelia; their ten-year-old daughter Ovita had not seen her father for nine years. Thomas had still not divorced his first wife Elizabeth, living in Salt Lake City with three of their four children. The second Mrs. Lloyd said that she was with her husband in Alaska before the expedition and since he had his doubts about Cook's claim, he decided to climb the mountain himself.

She didn't worry about him, if only because she'd grown accustomed to "these wild chases of his. When he kisses me goodbye I don't know whether he's going a hundred or a thousand miles . . . so I accepted his statement that he was going to the top of McKinley without question. He'd get there if he had to fly."

Thompson reinterpreted Mrs. Lloyd's interview from the April 14 *Star* as if he were citing facts rather than editorializing. In the *News Miner* on April 15, Thompson summarized the *Star* interview: "Mrs. Lloyd believes implicitly that her husband made the ascent of McKinley, declaring that if he says so it is so as he was always a truthful man."

Few readers would have noticed that Mrs. Lloyd never mentioned anything about her husband's truthfulness in the *Star* interview. (Within several years the couple divorced as Fairbanks readers would learn from another *News Miner* article, "Tom Lloyd Is Out of Trouble." Despite contempt of court charges leveled on him, Mrs. Lloyd's effort to collect alimony was initially denied because she filed in Seattle rather than Alaska.)

While most stateside papers ran the Fairbanks news about the sensational climb from the wire (ignoring or not seeing the gossipy *Star* story), Nebraska's *Lincoln Daily Star* wasn't buying it. On April 15, its editor wrote: "Since Thomas Lloyd has found that Cook did not reach the summit of Mt. McKinley, the world will wait for some other adventurer to discover that Lloyd didn't either. It may be necessary finally for all of us to go up and see the peak with our own eyes in order to avoid the suspicion that we are not being faked again."

The true believer W.F. Thompson tried to douse these flames. On that same day he printed the news about President Taft telegramming congratulations to Lloyd, "from one big man to another," for the successful ascent of Mt. McKinley. It was like Cook all over again: everyone wanted to believe Lloyd, so long as Thompson shrewdly promoted him as a humble, hayseed underdog rather than the big wheel-mining operator.

Thompson knew that a story with a credible sighting of Lloyd's six-by-twelve-foot flag flying from the fourteen-foot flagpole would help lay the groundwork for his big scoop, which they'd now sold to the *New York Times*. Despite Lloyd's original plan, a telescope in Fairbanks wouldn't do the job. Almost 150 miles away, the mountain, even from the highest hill in Fairbanks, still looked like a blurry dome cloud on the horizon. Clearly, the flagpole seen on the summit with a telescope as proof of the climb—backed by $1,500 of sponsorship from McPhee's Saloon—derived from too much whiskey talking.

Still, the press reported how one of many Lloyd disciples in Fairbanks, Dick Thorne, lugged his big telescope to the top of the tallest place, the town water tower. In hopes that the flag would turn broadside, Thorne eagerly but naively waited for a clear enough day to see Old Glory waving atop North America's highest mountain. "Almost ten times as much atmospheric mass," the mountaineer and later president of the University of Alaska Terris Moore wrote, "interposes between an observer at Fairbanks looking at the summit of McKinley as when he directs his telescope to a star overhead."

So Lloyd supporters scrapped the telescope verification. Three weeks after the climb, the *News Miner* printed a piece about John M. McLeod, who had just arrived in Fairbanks to tell another man's story: J.E. Baker had looked up through his binoculars from Kantishna at the mountain and on two different occasions, he saw the flag. Since McLeod had been suffering from snow blindness, he couldn't view the mountain. Also, Kantishna miners knew Thompson's story teller as "slightly unbalanced."

Thompson duly sent the detail-pumped story—sensationalized as if the Yeti had been sighted—out on the Associated Press wire. When the Utah papers figured out that it was their native son, Tom Lloyd ("The Utahn Man" one headline stated), even the *Salt Lake Herald* put a more upbeat spin on the story about Lloyd's "derring-do," chasing down the Robber's Roost gang, as if they had never doubted Lloyd for being bought out by Butch Cassidy back in 1897.

Later that month, newspapers around the country reprinted the interview of another skeptic, Charles Sheldon, the celebrated New York millionaire. Sheldon had wintered in the foothills of Denali (and would successfully lobby Congress to create a great park surrounding the mountain). Sheldon knew three of the four Sourdough climbers and two years earlier, on a hill above Lloyd's mining camp, had shown Lloyd the only feasible climbing route up the mountain's Muldrow Glacier.

In the interview, he called McGonagall and Taylor hardy young men and seasoned winter travelers who were courageous and capable. "None of the three, however, knows anything about technical mountain climbing," Sheldon said. "They have never seen an Alpine rope or an ice ax and are not familiar with technical mountaineering equipment."

There is "a great deal of public skepticism," Sheldon said, "particularly among those who are familiar with the hardships of mountain climbing." He sagely concluded that since Lloyd was the only one back out in civilization, the press should wait until the other climbers reemerged and verified their leader's story.

Privately, Sheldon then wrote to a friend: "Lloyd is a windbag and cannot climb. If he climbed McKinley (he is over 60 and fat and full of whiskey pickled in it) any 15 year old boy can do it."

The *News Miner* wrote that the Lloyd party's sponsors were preparing an article including twenty-five photographs of the climb. The article did not mention, however, that there were no publishable photos. Since a single photograph of the flagpole on top would obviously prove that they'd made the climb, in May, Lloyd sent a note to his "boys" in Kantishna that they needed to re-climb the mountain for more pictures, lest they be perceived as fakers like Cook.

The reading public hungered for these larger-than-life stories with pictures of their country's flag being planted on the most inaccessible and frozen corners of Earth. Still, it took a shrewd and skeptical reporter to ask the right questions of an adventurer. Then, even if these popular adventure stories were reported with consistent facts, many early-twentieth-century readers—more accustomed to reading the sports pages—had no context for judging what constituted an authentic expedition.

To this point, the Cook follies had generated a lot more ink than the story about Lloyd, who avoided the press. Still, even Cook's notoriety and press coverage would be eclipsed by his Norwegian friend Roald Amundsen or the Englishman Robert Scott in their preparations to reach the South Pole. (Scott's death there in 1911, despite being beaten to the pole by Amundsen, arguably sold more newspapers than any twentieth-century exploration on the planet.)

Amid a bullish American economy in 1910, newspapers like Thompson's *Miner* had become profitable powerhouses of advocacy. (Newspapermen today still call William F. Thompson one of Alaska's greatest "editorialists.") Conversely, while his paper vainly waxed optimistic about the local economy, the Alaskan gold rush era started trickling to an end—10 percent of Alaska's population began scurrying back south. Until that summer, Fairbanks was the biggest game in Alaska, with

3,500 residents, and thousands more bivouacked in mining camps as the gold began to play out and local banks failed. Kantishna's lagging gold production explained why Lloyd needed Fairbanks mountain-climbing cash sponsors in the first place: he had no money left to get his boys back out hunting for gold.

⌐⌐

With all of the contradictory press coverage, the lushly detailed 1910 *New York Times* scoop is the best summary of what the Sourdoughs might have done. "The First Account of the Conquering of Mount McKinley" hit the stands on June 5 as a three-page, uninterrupted opener for the Magazine section. The seventeen illustrations (half were photographs) included a pencil-drawn Pete Anderson in a striped parka, clutching a ten-foot-long hooked Shepherd's pole as if he were tending to a high-altitude flock, "planting the American flag on top of Mount McKinley" alongside a photograph of Lloyd in Chena on the outskirts of Fairbanks, after mushing in from his mining camp below Denali. A parka concealed his grape shape. Bowler-hatted men and a skimpy, four-dog sled team surrounded him. None of the photographs—reportedly posted in a metal tube and lost in the mail—showed the men climbing. Instead, Lloyd's diary and transcript of the expedition (from an interview performed by Thompson, of course, and recorded by a stenographer) described the climb.

According to that story, in January, the men waited in their cabins, unable to work their mining claims in the continuous subzero cold and darkness. Eventually, as the days grew longer and temperatures climbed to a more bearable twenty degrees below zero, they began preparing a route into the mountain.

Although Lloyd said nothing about it in print, other Alaskans talked of his fistfight with Charles Davidson, thirty-eight, who abruptly left before even reaching the mountain along with Billy Lloyd (no relation to Tom) and Bob Horne. Tom Lloyd claimed Davidson's knee was bothering him. With neither a confirming black eye nor limp, these stories—like the bet that might've started their climb—show the thick veil of mythos still surrounding their feat.

Thompson's introductory narrative continued, "and the four old 'Tillicums' made the climb alone." Unfortunately, Davidson, later surveyor general of Alaska, was the only one who could work the barometer and $5 Kodak camera.

Lloyd, Anderson, McGonagall, and Taylor spent another month breaking trail, bridging crevasses and load ferrying to what they called fifteen thousand feet (actually eleven thousand feet). Here they pitched their last bivouac—called "Tunnel Camp"—inside a large snow cave to keep their tent from blowing away or collapsing under the weight of snowfall. Then they began working the ridge above. Since wind-driven snow filled in the steps, over the ensuing days, they repeatedly climbed up and cleaned out the steps.

As working-class men of the northern frontier, rather than gentlemen alpinists, they lacked ice axes. Their long, spiked pike poles weren't even eighteenth-century batons or alpenstocks—as they were called in France or Germany. As working class, flatlanders oblivious to alpine tools, they chose to take pike poles, used by fire fighters or lumberjacks. Instead of pulling down burning buildings or moving logs in a river, they would jam the hooked tops into the snow to arrest a fall or provide a handrail. Otherwise they were deployed for balance, as a third leg. Lacking the essential adze found on ice axes, they carried wood hatchets. To chop steps, the hatchets had to be swung in awkward, horizontal arcs.

Since Karstens Ridge was mostly snow, rather than the ice found up higher, they spent days digging. They used their long-handled coal shovel to sculpt a 3,600-foot miner's staircase up the mountain's spine. Except for the thin air and unnerving chasms at their feet, the labor taxed them no more than damming huge streams, building sluices, or digging tunnels in Kantishna or the Klondike, work that they believed would have crippled a Cheechako grandee like Cook, who lived in a turreted Brooklyn mansion.

In the context of world exploration up to 1910 and for decades remaining, their feat, if they really did it, would stand as the most difficult high mountain route yet climbed. Unlike other wealthy sportsmen of the Edwardian Era, these blue-collar Alaskan conquerors—with the exception of packing loads up and over the steep Chilkoot Pass from the Alaskan seashore into Canada and the Klondike—had zero mountaineering experience. Even Cook had at least scrambled on polar glaciers and up small peaks, or followed his horse packer's chopped steps a few thousand feet up McKinley.

Blithely unaware of and freed from alpine conventions, wearing the same stiffened canvas and malodorous wool used on the trail, the Sourdoughs worked the mountain as if digging for the mother lode. The millions of newspaper readers—from London to New York to Wichita, let alone skeptical alpinists from Canada to Nepal—would not understand that, if truthful, these amateur and unknown climbers were ushering in a new style of speedy climbing. (Their "alpine-style" sprint up and down more than eight thousand feet in eighteen hours, without using fixed camps, took place a half century before the

Ubermensch climbers from the Alps even attempted moving so boldly at high altitude.)

After Thompson's bombastic introduction to Lloyd, his June 5 *Times* interview (reprinted in the following day's *London's Daily Telegraph*) captured Lloyd's plainspoken speech to Thompson and the stenographer. This followed with three months' worth of dated entries purported to be copied from Lloyd's diary (which conveniently disappeared after this interview). Beginning in February and detailing two months' worth of approach from the frozen tundra up onto the glacier, the April 1 entry read: "I started this morning for the summit to join the other boys for the final climb. . . . It snowed a little last night, and it was as foggy as it could be this morning, but I pulled out so as to leave enough wood here for our use when we return from the summit. This evening I joined the boys in the Tunnel Camp, but it was pretty late in the evening."

The next day, according to Lloyd, they left Tunnel Camp at dawn and summited the South Peak by 3 p.m.—an extraordinarily fast time for such a large altitude gain. He noted that the twin North Peak two miles away looked to be the same height. (From their mining camps, the North Peak looks taller, but the more distant South Peak is 840 feet higher.)

On the South Peak, they couldn't find any rocks to raise the flagpole. So to appease the sponsors back in Fairbanks, according to Lloyd, they decided to erect the flagpole on the rocky North Peak the following day.

His diary reads that they left before daylight again on April 3. Even a century ago, readers would have seen this as an incredible act of endurance, summiting with such an enormous altitude gain on two consecutive days. This time they were dragging and lugging the flagpole to Denali Pass, an

18,200-foot saddle between the two peaks (modern climbers believe that they turned off the Harper Glacier at 16,000 feet, to the more difficult and direct Sourdough Couloir).

Even in these so-called diary entries, Lloyd repeatedly mentions and praises his teammates. "Anderson kept the time," he wrote, "as my watch had gone on the bum, and I can get the time we made from him—didn't think of it when I left, never dreaming that our story would be printed, or desiring that it should."

Atop the North Peak, Lloyd said that they built a rock monument that would "endure as long as the top of the mountain does . . . although the rocks were hard for us to dig out in that altitude. The snow filled in between the rocks, and they were frozen together, but we dug down 15 inches into the rocks until we had found a solid spot."

They attached the huge flag onto their spruce sapling— four inches at the butt, tapering to two and a half inches at the top—and raised it so that all of Fairbanks could see it through the telescope. If Lloyd thought the flagpole had been a burden on any of the steep sections, or along the knife-edged Karstens Ridge, he didn't mention it. He did add a patriotic flourish about the "flag erected by four Americans of Welsh, Scotch, Canadian and Swedish descent" (omitting that Taylor and Anderson had not yet obtained citizenship). Nor did Lloyd fail to mention the sponsor's name, written on the flag in ink, "E.W. Griffin."

Anderson apparently took a picture of his companions, but according to Lloyd, failed to fully slide open the lever on their Kodak camera. They nailed a wooden board to the flagpole, dated and inscribed: "Lloyd Party. Pioneers of Alaska. William H. McPhee, Gust Peterson, Pete Anderson, Charles McGonagall, W.R. Taylor, T. Lloyd."

Lloyd abruptly ended his excerpted diary: "That is the story of our climb." The more astute *New York Times* readers—navigating through this chronologically adrift, shaggy dog tale—would've wondered whether these diary entries were authentic. The narrative felt more like bar talk than terse scribbling from inside subzero tents (many years later, Taylor told an interviewer that Lloyd's diary comprised only brief notes jotted down in a tiny memorandum booklet designed for a vest pocket).

That Sunday's *Times* edition, including Lloyd's account, ran seventy-two pages long, but no story came close to competing with either the narrative or illustrations contained in the McKinley piece. If Lloyd worried about readers believing him, at least on the far-off east coast, unlike northern Alaska, no one could see his aging, sumo-wrestler proportions.

"The trouble with me, principally," Lloyd said, starting candid, yet finishing with an exaggeration: "was that I was mostly too fat for climbing mountains, but I lost thirty pounds on the trip."

Since Lloyd had learned the value of a creating a loyal posse to get ahead in life, he told Thompson and the stenographer that his companions were far superior to him during the climb or on the flats. "They did the work, before and behind," he said, "and I kept camp." Still, with narcissism remarkably similar to Cook's, Lloyd heaped credit on himself for picking men capable of the climb.

As for Anderson, "the Swede," Lloyd called him a world's wonder, with nearly unlimited endurance, "a tower of strength." Inferring that the altitude didn't faze the Swede, he talked of how they breathed through opened mouths because their nostrils alone wouldn't "serve any one of us for *windgetting*."

Of the strong-as-a-horse Taylor, he proved more than adequate for the task of building the rock monument that held their flagpole. They called him Billy for his youthfulness, but they respected him for his business acumen, establishing a profitable horse and dogsled freighting business out of Fairbanks.

During the descent over one particularly steep section, Lloyd described how Taylor slipped and slid with alarming speed down the snow. Praising his quick thinking, Lloyd said that Taylor wisely didn't dig in his creepers—which would've flipped him like a rag doll and potentially broken his legs as the spikes caught. Instead, he performed what trained mountaineers called a "self arrest": digging the hooked end of his antediluvian pole into the snow until he came slowly to a stop two hundred feet later at the brink of a dizzying drop down to the Tralieka Glacier.

Lloyd concluded that the chasm was so high that there wouldn't have been a "grease spot" left of Taylor when he hit bottom. At this point in the story, whether a reader believed Lloyd or not was immaterial, because he could colorfully stretch a Bunyanesque yarn. Beside, with alpinism in its infancy, when even "armchair mountaineers" were unheard-of, most readers wouldn't have been able to discern up from down in this story.

Inside this tall tale, Lloyd issued at least one statement that, to an experienced alpinist, could explain how they might have pulled off this futuristic climb. Lloyd called the route something that men couldn't climb, emphasizing the limitation of early snow and ice craft: on steepening slopes, climbers had to chop steps with their ice axes so that their primitive, four-pointed creepers would hold. Then Lloyd continued as if their creepers were something different: "you can climb ice walls just as you can go up a telegraph pole." Instead of step-chopping up slightly angled mountainsides he was referring to cleats that linemen wore on their boots to climb straight up—the same devices Butch Cassidy's gang used to climb a pole and cut the telegraph line out of Castle Gate, Utah, after the robbery.

Even if Lloyd amplified the steepness of their climb or the magic of their creepers, his team may have been onto something unprecedented in alpinism: no one had yet climbed mountains like pole linemen. Also, when it came to glacier travel, arduous trailbreaking, and avoidance of falling through crevasse bridges (softened by warmer temperatures), he made accurate observations. "In this trip we were always praying for the thermometer to drop, so that it couldn't snow any more and the trail could not soften," Lloyd said. "We didn't want any weather above zero."

Given his remark about optimal cold conditions and the innovative and essential creepers potentially being used like more modern crampons, and in light of the fact that their climb was so far beyond the difficulty of other mountain routes in 1910, a modern-day reader could be forgiven for wanting to believe Lloyd.

Near the story's end, after praising the creepers, Lloyd praised Charlie McGonagall. His reputation, Lloyd said, preceded him throughout the region for driving the mail on dogsled throughout ghastly winters. "[He] was a wonderful fellow."

Lloyd related the story of how McGonagall took a short cut off their broken trail across the badly crevassed glacier. When a hidden crevasse bridge broke beneath his feet, he fell into his waist and caught himself with his long, hooked pole

(McGonagall designed it, then had a Fairbanks blacksmith make the poles and creepers). After McGonagall threw himself off the pole and out of the crevasse, nimble as a cat, he never took another shortcut again.

Throughout the narrative, Lloyd repeatedly mentioned the Swede. When the Welshman thought they were about to perish in an avalanche inside their tent, the frozen river of ice briefly shifting underneath their caribou mattresses, he jumped up. "But the Swede, who had crossed many glaciers, paid no attention at all. He simply looked at me and smiled and said, 'It's just rippling a little below; it is safe here.'"

The Swede had frozen his toes before the climb to the summit but carried on without complaint. By trip's end, at least one of his toes had developed a bulbous, frostbite blister—"during the last few weeks it bled something fierce every night" after he repeatedly banged his toes against his boots while stepkicking.

Somehow Anderson continued climbing up, then walking out. Lloyd was not exaggerating in saying that the Swede "suffered the tortures of the damned." Or that the whole climb was "simply a matter of endurance."

Lloyd rambled on about recycling their grounds when the coffee ran out, or the value of using copper kettles, or that he was sending samples of summit rocks to the Smithsonian for analysis, and how black their skin had turned after being burnt by the sun. He also expressed his wish—given their lack of pictures—that a photographer should have accompanied them, neglecting to mention that he had already punched his photographer right out of the expedition. And as expected, he mused about Cook, saying that since the Cheechako didn't mention using snowshoes, that he couldn't possibly have made the climb.

Oddly, Lloyd mentioned nothing about Cook's lack of creepers, which the Sourdoughs found so essential to their climb.

For a Welshman as worldly and ambitious as the gentile sheriff and state mine inspector who hit pay dirt in the Klondike, the narration feels disjointed, lacking in even the simplest metaphors, analogies, or concluding remarks. Compared to the erudite and detailed mining reports that Lloyd regularly submitted to Utah's governor, the *Times* story painted Lloyd as a simpleton. Yet, this was exactly how Thompson wanted his subject to be perceived—a more articulate hero could have been perceived as pulling the wool over his reader's eyes. "It is a 'roughneck' story," Thompson wrote in the Introduction (avoiding embellished language or a portrait that might evoke the haughty Cook), "told by a roughneck pioneer, who will not believe that he has done anything worthy of "making a fuss over."

Lloyd ended the interview section of the story with more praise of Anderson: "Mount McKinley must be 21,000 feet high, but that Swede is a wonder," Lloyd said. "If it was twice as high as it is I believe the Swede could go to the top of it."

As that story hit the newsstands, two more Cheechako expeditions had already entered the race behind the unbelievable Sourdoughs, attempting Denali from the south, retracing Cook's route up the Ruth Glacier. The first, led by Claude Rusk, was the Mazamas expedition out of Seattle, sponsored by newspapers that had backed Cook in the past. Rusk, at first, was inclined to believe Cook—but not Lloyd.

Outside of the Alaska Range, Rusk met an unnamed Fairbanks pioneer who knew Lloyd. Rusk later wrote about this meeting, recorded in his diary, for the *Overland Journal*: "I wouldn't believe [Lloyd] under oath. He can't travel 10 miles a day on [flat] ground." Dispensing the ultimate Alaskan insult, the pioneer railed that Lloyd couldn't even hunt his own meat.

The other expedition (from the Explorer's Club that had recently disbarred Cook as a member) motored swiftly upriver. It was led by Cook's former teammates, the personable Belmore Browne and the scholarly Hershel Parker. During this race to climb Denali, they easily passed Rusk's team in their powerful motor launch the *Explorer*—its engine so loud they called it the *Exploder*. Rusk and company were slowly, awkwardly poling their motorless boat upstream on the Chulitna River, embarrassed as the *Explorer* thundered past them, then pissed off as the wake rocked their subpar scow.

First on the Explorers Club's agenda would be to find what Browne and Parker were calling "Fake Peak," which they believed Cook had used as a phony "studio" to represent the top of the continent. Their plan: to replicate Cook's "summit" photograph and show the world that the 1906 climb was a hoax.

Up on the Ruth Glacier, a month underway, miles from the nearest greenery, their sleuthing paid off. By lining up distant peaks seen in Cook's image, Browne and Parker found a bump on a ridge: 5,338 feet high and 15 miles away from the 20,310-foot summit of Denali. He and Parker quickly scrambled three hundred feet above the glacier. While their teammate Herman Tucker held out a flag on top, Browne exposed an image that matched Cook's *To the Top of the Continent* photograph.

After this, Rusk's and Browne's teams met once, convivially, as they moved up-glacier. But they came to an abrupt halt beneath Denali's imposing south and east buttresses rising steeply off the Ruth Glacier (unclimbed for the next forty-four and fifty-three years, respectively), guarded by enormous crevasses and swept by avalanches. Both teams were stronger, better outfitted, and more experienced climbers than Cook and Barrill. Plus, the 1910 climbers carried the creepers that Parker was certain that Cook lacked. While Rusk's team ran out of food and left, Browne and Parker spent several more weeks probing every ridge and ramp, until all possibilities were exhausted as feasible climbs. There was simply no way that Cook could have done it in less than two weeks in one go with packs under fifty pounds.

Rusk concluded in his *Overland Journal* article that Cook did not climb McKinley. "That is all for Dr. Cook. . . . As he sowed so has he reaped. If he is mentally unbalanced, he is entitled to the pity of mankind. If he is not, there is no corner of the earth where he can hide from his past."

By now Cook had been all but disrobed. In the absence of these two Cheechako expeditions that summer of 1910, a story entitled "Cook Tried to Steal Parson's Life Work" appeared in the *New York Times*. It concerned the Yahgan dictionary that Cook borrowed in 1898 from the Bridges family in Tierra del Fuego while returning from Antarctica. Cook, after transcribing the Anglican Minister Thomas Bridges's private alphabet into English, tried to publish the work under his own name. As an amateur ethnologist, spending only six weeks in the region treating sick Ona patients, Cook pretended that he had studied the nearby Yahgan tribe (whom he had scarcely seen) and learned enough of their language to compile a dictionary. For the rest of Lucas Bridges's (son of Thomas) life, he continued sending letters to Cook demanding that the original manuscript be returned. Cook never complied.

If he'd maintained the integrity of his early explorations, his scientific contributions might have been remembered. Aside from being a compassionate physician, he had repeatedly observed and written about the Inuit in northern Greenland. In Alaska, unlike most single-minded mountaineers, Cook had carefully spent time with and noted how southern tribes revered Raven and his creation of Denali. But his dishonest explorations began to taint everything that he touched.

That fall, the *New York Times* published Browne's replicated Cook summit photograph. Under the headline "Explodes Dr. Cook's Mt. M'Kinley Claim," the Barrill affidavit was mentioned, while Parker and Browne dismissed Cook's climb to the top of North America.

At about this time, Robert Dunn, the *Shameless Diary* author, ran into Cook at the Waldorf. "Hey, Doc. Put it all over on the world, didn't you? I greeted him." They talked, Dunn wrote in his autobiography, for an hour. "Whether or not he believed what he said, I couldn't tell, but his justification of his claims grew pathetic."

Peary received a pension from the US Navy and a congressional-presidential decree for being first to reach the North Pole. Cook—once cheered by tens of thousands on his return from the pole in 1909—tried to rally support through his lecture tours. Then he disappeared.

He reemerged in the west, working as a geologist in Wyoming, then as a promoter of oil lands in Texas. Since the lands he sold through the mail were initially deemed worthless, in 1923, he was convicted for mail fraud and sentenced to five years in Leavenworth. He served an additional two years while trying to appeal the conviction.

Throughout this ordeal, he maintained his innocence (he was later pardoned by President Roosevelt when the same oil lands were found to be profitable) as well as his claims to have reached the pole and the top of the continent. In August 1940, he fell into a coma and as his lungs filled with fluid, he died of pulmonary edema—a common high-altitude affliction for Denali climbers. It took until 1989 for a rigorous analysis of the navigational data of Robert Peary (who died in 1920) to discredit his claim to the North Pole. While both men are generally considered to be expedition hoaxers, an ardent coterie of armchair mountaineers known as the Frederick Cook Society continues to defend their hero's claims to both Denali and the pole.

~~

In 1910, Parker gave a New York Explorer's Club lecture that gently debunked Cook—a gentleman from the same city—by calling his Denali fraudulence "a glorious failure." Earlier in the year, he commented about the rougher-edged Alaskan miner Lloyd. "From what I read of Lloyd's account," Parker told an Alaskan reporter, "it's just as probable that Lloyd reached the summit as that Cook reached the pole."

Browne had chimed in to the same reporter that the saloonkeeper and gambler, McPhee, had backed Lloyd. McPhee, according to Browne, had told Lloyd to come back with either the peak or the story. "Why," Browne said, "everyone knows that Lloyd had been dead broke for a year, waiting for someone to grubstake him. All those fellows have dog teams, so the trip probably stood them only a couple hundred dollars."

(Browne's trip—from the east coast, to the Alaska seashore, thence ninety miles upriver in a modern speedboat—cost ten times as much.) Parker concluded to this reporter that it was an "absolute impossibility" to carry a "16-foot" flagpole to the summit of Mt. McKinley. When the perennial gamblers of Fairbanks heard this, Griffin and the embezzling founder of Fairbanks, E.T. Barnett, offered a $100,000 bet that Lloyd did make it to the summit. To prove it, the gamblers said, Lloyd would guide the professor back up the mountain.

But this "bespectacled highbrow" hardly needed Lloyd's help. Parker and Browne knew the mountain better than any Sourdough and were already planning a rematch. This time, they planned to climb Lloyd's northern route. They were as interested in disproving Cook as the Sourdoughs were—even though their duplicated photograph of the doctor's photograph from atop "fake peak," surrounded by higher mountains, should've been the final nail in his coffin.

—◡—

Earlier that summer, several days after Lloyd's *New York Times* story broke, McGonagall, Taylor, and Anderson put down their pickaxes and boated out the Kantishna River, turned down the Bearpaw's current and reached Fairbanks by the Tanana. In the summer, after the ice broke from these rivers, their downstream journey from the mines took only three days.

The next day's *News Miner* ran yet another startling piece about the three men climbing the Southern Peak of the mountain a second time. In May, according to the reporter, they had rushed up the mountain nonstop in three days and took pictures of the summit and flag. Although wrapped around the pole, the flag was "as good as it ever was, unaffected by the winds or storms." This new claim—beating their already speedy April ascent—ran in more newspapers around the country, serving as a strategic bolstering of the *New York Times* story. Still, the growing skepticism about these prodigious feats would have been quickly dispelled if the Lloyd–McKinley Committee produced actual photographic proof.

So they did the next best thing. On June 11, knowing how Barrill's affidavit in the New York newspapers had recently cooked Cook's goose, they all signed a notarized affidavit that on April 3 all four of them had planted their pole on the North Summit and "at the hour of three twenty-five o'clock p.m. unfurl[ed] a United States flag." Unlike Barrill, since Lloyd was their employer and business partner, they signed in deference to their boss without being paid. The affidavit, of course, did not mention their phenomenal May repeat climb, nor their supposed April climb to the South Summit, despite what had been printed in the *Miner* two days earlier, despite the *New York Times* photograph marking that peak— rather than the North Summit—with a circle as the site of the flag-planting.

If Lloyd was prevaricating and contradicting himself, as some of his Fairbanks friends suspected, tall tales in the northern frontier were ingrained into the subculture, inspiring pioneers to dig to the mother lode—or climb to the top of the continent—through toughness and self-sufficiency alone.

Also, conquering Denali's South Summit versus its twin, the North Peak, struck those who had never climbed a mountain as an irrelevant abstraction. *Who cared if one peak was slightly higher than the other?*

Along with the affidavit, Lloyd and his sponsors McPhee, Peterson, and Griffin—the Lloyd–Mt. McKinley Committee and charter members of the Pioneers of Alaska—shrewdly arranged several group portraits in Harry Huey's Fairbanks studio. One version of this arresting image shows the three climbers standing around their leader, Lloyd, enthroned like Alaskan nobility, on a well-varnished armchair, concealing his rotundity. While Lloyd's face was pale the others were bronzed from the mountain sun. All were dressed in their Sunday best, although suits and ties had to be rented for all but Lloyd, whose jacket needed pressing. Unaccustomed to formal dress, they neglected to cinch ties up to their shirt tops. Billy Taylor rested his right hand on Tom Lloyd's shoulder with unmistakable (albeit temporary) solidarity. Despite their backwoodsman reputations, the celluloid pose deftly converted them into trustworthy looking gentlemen. They didn't live in East Coast mansions but they presented as honorable-enough fellows.

Over the next century, the portrait would be reprinted in countless publications around the world. Lloyd, ever wary of outside media, still saw fit to mail this dapper photograph of him leading the posse to the *Salt Lake Tribune*, where his sheriff's star first began to shine. On August 28, 1910, the image of the former "Salt Laker" and his friends monopolized the front page. "There is no Utahn who doubts the word of Tom Lloyd," the story caption read. "When he stated that he climbed to the summit of Mt. McKinley, that settled it. He did."

The Fairbanks Four portrait bore remarkable similarity to another classic image—shot just ten years earlier—of the Sundance Kid and the Wild Bunch in similar three-piece suits, standing with hands resting on the shoulders of Butch Cassidy, relaxing in an armchair. Butch personally sent that portrait, along with a thank you note to the Nevada bank they'd just robbed.

For Alaskans, Lloyd was also a patriot, a gentile sheriff among fanatics and a gunslinger who hunted down the most notorious outlaw in America. More importantly to Fairbanks—a gold-mining settlement in the midst of a precipitous financial decline, rapidly losing its citizenry and on the verge of becoming a ghost town—Lloyd's feat helped pin the northernmost city on the map and in the national news. Fairbanks needed him. Besides, the man had lived out the fantasy of every Sourdough who could recite a Robert Service ballad—Lloyd had struck it rich (or maybe lost a fortune) in Nome, Kantishna, and the Klondike.

As Service wrote:

There are strange things done,
In the midnight sun
By the men who moil for gold.

on the slope of
Mt. McGinley

The Sourdoughs McGonagall and Lloyd wielding pike poles at 11,000 feet on the Muldrow Glacier. McGonagall's unlined, cotton mattress-ticking parka is filthy, while Lloyd's appears unused.
ALASKA STATE LIBRARY, HISTORICAL COLLECTIONS, P277-004-089?

Karstens in 1914 below Denali, clad in state-of-the-art mattress-ticking parka over wool sweaters, flannel shirts, and bib overalls with wolverine ruff and moose-hide mittens—same as the 1910 Sourdough outfits.
KARSTENS FAMILY COLLECTION

The Cheechako Cook in 1917
as a retired explorer, recently
plunged into the oil business.
LIBRARY OF CONGRESS, PRINTS &
PHOTOGRAPHS DIVISION, PHOTOGRAPH
BY HARRIS & EWING

ENLARGED POLE 18,500 FEET

SOURDOUGH
COULOIR

In 1912, at 18,000 feet, the Cheechako Merl LaVoy exposed this two-mile
distant view of the North Peak's shoulder, unknowingly photographing the route
taken by the 1910 Sourdoughs and a flagpole invisible to the naked eye.
PAPERS OF BELMORE BROWNE, RAUNER SPECIAL COLLECTIONS LIBRARY AT DARTMOUTH
COLLEGE

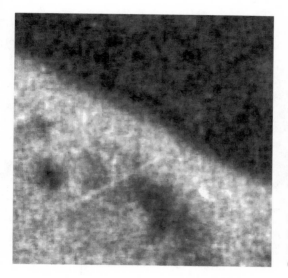

The Sourdough mystery is solved by zooming in 400x to LaVoy's photograph, unveiling the flagpole in the last rocks of the couloir, partially highlighted against the sky (the white diagonal line is a scratch).

Gunnar Naslund balancing up Karstens Ridge in 1977 with the awkward 14-foot spruce pole during an attempted re-creation of the 1910 Sourdough climb.

(Left to right) McGonagall, Lloyd, Anderson, and Taylor in June 1910
Fairbanks portrait taken to help the miners stake their claim to Denali.
DENALI NATIONAL PARK

South and north peak on right, with Karstens Ridge center, to the left of
Harper Icefall and Glacier. The Sourdough Couloir is just visible in sunlight
leading up to the Pioneer Ridge.
TOM FALLEY PHOTOGRAPH

Arthur Aten with sled dogs and caribou on the tundra below Denali, on the
Parker-Cheechako expedition, May 2012.

Lloyd in Fairbanks with his heavyweight drinking buddies and old-timer Pioneers
in 1911.

The Pioneer Ridge leading from top of Sourdough Couloir (not seen) to North Peak (19,470 feet); South Summit (20,310 feet) behind.
TOM FALLEY PHOTOGRAPH

Park Service helicopter evacuation of the deceased climber Masayuki Ikeda from 14,300 feet on the West Buttress, June 2016.
JON WATERMAN PHOTOGRAPH

Climbers with sleds starting up the elegant Karstens Ridge, with Browne's Tower above.
BRIAN OKONEK PHOTOGRAPH

Denali National Park was the first park established after the formation of the National Park Service. These homemade crampons were used by the 1910 Sourdough Expedition. With hot chocolate, donuts, and a 14-foot spruce pole, they became the first to summit Denali's 19,470-foot north peak.

Ingenious, nine-point, galvanized steel crampons (the first in North America) used on 1910 climb, recovered on Muldrow Glacier in 1932.
JON WATERMAN PHOTOGRAPH

The three-page *New York Times* Magazine cover story of June 5, 1910, with the hyperbolic Lloyd account.
THE NEW YORK TIMES

The author's companions Inman, Hutchins, Cosker, Hamilton, and Fraser flying out to Talkeetna, June 2016.
JON WATERMAN PHOTOGRAPH

Interlude: June 2016

As we climbed higher, one step at a time above Denali Pass on my sixtieth birthday, I chased after a rhythm. This struggle to reach the top felt more than familiar, like a dance step imbued to both ligature and cerebral cortex.

Between the reassuring cornflake-crunch of crampons penetrating ice, the silence atop North America is profound. While above all the clamor and movement in the green world below, up high—for the moment anyway, without storm—it registered as white and otherworldly peace. A place apart. The North Peak beckoned behind, almost more than the South Peak called to me above, hidden behind the stubby granite of Archdeacon's Tower. My crampons continued to squeak into hard snow and crack ice as I clomped and weighted each foot.

Sixty years old, for much of my culture, signaled retirement time. Yet, I had come for different reasons: to understand my Sourdough heroes, reconnect to a mountain that had offered direction and profound meaning to my life, and now, to move forward in a new beginning. It occurred to me that, in Asia, sixtieth birthdays are celebrated as rebirths. According to the Chinese Zodiac calendar—as I swung and crunched toward outer space—the planets were aligned in the exact same place as the day I was born sixty long years ago. If it meets your needs, I figured, even skeptics could swear by their horoscope.

Although I didn't normally consult the *I Ching*, read the tea leaves, or visit psychics, I had a lot to look forward to. For starters, I no longer had to worry about hitting midlife crisis. And soon, as my sons grew into adults and took on the world, I would watch them change it with pride.

From this viewpoint of being a water bottle half full, committed to the climb, I expected to kick into high gear. Despite panting I was warm and fit, barely sweating.

I lifted my feet high and clear, bent my ankles, and without scraping or catching the ice with my twelve sharpened crampon points, I stomped the points down flatfooted, gently, firmly, again and again. On the steeps I stood straight and tall and resisted the urge to lean in and crutch with my short ax. I lost myself to the cadence of breath, my lungs unstoppable bellows, my heart a powerful pump.

While each step hurt, it felt a mere discomfort in the way that marathon runners welcome the last mile of unthinking animal response. Pre-trip training had taught me how to hit the wall and then continue so long as I stayed hydrated and took in calories every hour. Valves expanded and shrunk; blood rushed in and out despite scant oxygen; lungs inflated and contracted. My pulse hung at something like 140 beats per minute. This, my aged performance, if not a surprise to me, did impress my teammates. These young, otherwise nonplussed rope mates—especially the long-suffering Cory Inman, now holding his head—were flummoxed that someone twice their age could keep the pace. Moreover, they depended upon my hard-won knowledge of this mountain, the time I had logged in storm, the peculiar connections I had made with granite and ice scraping up toward oxygen-deprived stratosphere. Or so I supposed.

This high on the continent, nearing the tropospheric ceiling, the air felt clean, even light as I gulped it in and out, in and out. Except for the bite of steel points into ice and a mild whisper of wind, the silence reigned. In brief lifts of cloud that allowed the sun to throw shadows, the light too was pure, but without heat against my skin. I pulled the silk balaclava up over my lips and laughed at the cold. The weather was holding.

I belonged here, I told myself, half believing it.

Still, I no longer felt old. Not dizzy or hurting or scared, but aligned with the mountain. I became muscle fiber and deep breath and bestial willpower and lucid memory. A human metronome, lost to the pace. The response of my body—like most high-altitude climbers fighting the last slope on autopilot—allowed my thoughts to travel back in time. I recalled being young here in a past that seemed like another lifetime:

I am nineteen, dressed in army surplus wool clothing, a cotton-nylon anorak and steel-shanked leather double boots with cinched-tight crampon straps numbing my toes, but at nineteen thousand feet the altitude pounds like a drum in my head and I knew we had no chance of making the last thousand feet but swear I'll come back and do it right next time.

I am twenty-four, after a tandem solo sprint up the West Rib Route with my partner (still five hundred feet below) as I nap alone on the summit with my Gore-tex bibbed legs and plastic boots hanging out over the abyss of the south face; I have the summit to myself and the mountain feels like an animate being, the air rising and falling on all of North America below and me hanging onto the world as one big animal beneath me.

I am twenty-five, unroped and alone, haunted by lethal winter while crawling for my life, clad in a Thinsulate suit and three layers of mittens, to the top of the Cassin Ridge in what seems to be outer space at 20,100 feet with the clouds a clean white blanket ready to catch me before hitting the earth far below, but I keep on with fluid-filled lungs and frostbitten toes, so afraid to stop that I will fight all day and night in exchange for just being able to survive.

I am twenty-eight, but unable to try for the summit after our exhaustive high-altitude rescue—a five-thousand-foot, mid-night lower of a broken-legged Japanese climber—as we cross over Denali Pass from the west buttress and carve telemark turns down the Harper Glacier through newly fallen powder snow past the Sourdough Couloir: guarded by blue water ice and a large bergschrund that looks impossible for ill-equipped century-old pioneers.

I am thirty-seven, with a television film crew and friends walking two feet below the summit, circling warily because I will never top out again and then the camera and sound mike are running and I speak the words rehearsed all the way up Karstens Ridge:

We don't climb mountains for the sake of conquest, but to celebrate all the world below, so I will stop short of putting Denali beneath my crampons and pay respects to this mountain as part of a greater wilderness below.

Over the last quarter century, I thought a lot about that below-the-summit speech. This sixtieth year of realigned planets day, I picked up my pace, spurred on by anger as I remembered that those words were not the only moments that got cut from my hour-long ESPN "Surviving Denali" documentary.

At the beginning of our 1993 film journey, we hired a Tena (Athapaskan) to read a script about Denali's Creation from the Distant Time. On a cloudless day, the mountain glowing bright white like an unearthly orb on the horizon, we filmed this man on the edge of Cook Inlet, as if to visualize waves turning into mountains. But the Athapaskan didn't need the script and recited his own version of the Sacred Story from memory. He emphasized that this tale should not be confused with fairy tales, legends, or myths.

His story went like this:

Yako the Demigod of great powers wanted a bride but lived alone in a land without humans. After he caulked his canoe and paddled to a distant village, Yako took his young bride Tsukala away across an inland sea, pursued by the Raven chief Totson who used his magic and created a storm with huge green waves to swamp and drown Yako. As the waves grew higher and stronger, Totson threw a great spear at Yako, who turned the tallest wave into a mountain—catching the spear on its top—as Totson crashed his canoe into the mountain now known as Denali, the High One, and turned into a raven. Tsukala and Yako then became man and wife, and their children populated the land as the Tena people.

Over my protests, the editor cut out the Tena's Sacred Story. Amid the Emmy Award–winning cinematography of our 1993 pioneer style traverse, done without airplane support, the film included footage of a 1932 park service expedition, flailing with skis on the Muldrow Glacier. We also included footage of the famed mountaineer Brad Washburn on the summit with his wife, Barbara, kissing one another next to that four-foot pole flying a flag in 1947.

But stuck in my mind during this 2016 summit attempt remained one more piece of missing history. Since the Sourdoughs had taken no pictures of their 1910 ascent and flagpole, the film we made neglected to mention their unbelievable climb. High time, I figured, even if I wouldn't top out on this one last climb, to set the record straight about Lloyd, Anderson, Taylor, and McGonagall.

PART II

January 1911

Whether a believer or a coconspirator in Fairbanks Fake News, in January 1911, under "TOM LLOYD IS HIKING TO EAST," Thompson ran a curious and short paragraph in the *News Miner*. Lloyd believed that the rocks that he gathered from McKinley's summit, sent to the Smithsonian Institute, got mixed up, which he would attempt to rectify. And while back east, the article said, he would try to meet with Professor Parker.

Lloyd never made it back east. Later that month, however, he debarked from an Alaska steamship in Seattle and embraced another woman instead of his second wife. Mrs. Lloyd, formerly Emelia Peterson, bore witness to this betrayal. Heartbroken yet again, she filed divorce papers. She would tell the court that, a year earlier, Lloyd had abandoned her and forced her, in destitution, to take a Fairbanks hotel job so that she could return to their child in Seattle.

During this visit, a reporter from the *Seattle Times* corralled Lloyd for a lengthy puff piece. Impressed by Lloyd's "modern Hercules" physique, the writer described "a chest like a flour barrel, doubtless developed from breathing the thin air of high altitudes and cold temperatures."

At first, Lloyd provided noncommunicative, monosyllabic answers about the climb. Then when the reporter told Lloyd he deserved the lion's share of the credit, he sat up and called McGonagall the real hero of the expedition.

Lloyd expanded on what he'd said for the *New York Times* article about the creepers McGonagall invented. Like Thompson, the reporter emphasized Lloyd's modesty and his quiet, matter-of-fact tone as he rambled on about the creepers being the secret to their climb. As a non-climber with a lay audience that wouldn't understand technical equipment, the reporter instead turned to the perennial question of why anyone would want to climb a mountain.

Lloyd replied that it wasn't for glory for themselves or for science. As the consummate promoter, he then waved the Sourdough flag: "The Pioneers of Alaska wanted to show that if anybody could make the ascent it would be the men who were used to the life of the Northland."

That summer, Browne and Parker returned to Alaska. This time, they delayed their Denali climbing attempt to prospect for gold in the southeast part of the state. But the yellow metal eluded them.

Since news of their upcoming attempt had already hit the papers, Lloyd's Pioneers of Alaska buddy E.W. Griffin wired Professor Parker a request that, in case he made it to the top of Mt. McKinley during his expedition, he needed to bring down the flag that Lloyd placed on the north summit. Griffin mentioned that Lloyd would make a trip to the bottom of the mountain to watch Parker's climb.

Griffin's round-faced, Roman-nosed portrait had appeared in the previous year's *New York Times* exclusive along with images of the other "Pioneer Sponsors" Peterson and McPhee. It seemed unbelievable that there were no photographs of the unpaid climbers Anderson, Taylor, or McGonagall. Adding insult to injury, The *Times* had also rewarded the sponsors with several hundred dollars as part of Thompson's contract for the exclusive.

In cahoots with Thompson, Griffin had written Parker as part of a promotional *News Miner* story to plug both the Fairbanks Pioneers and his Chena mercantile store, seven miles outside of Fairbanks, by mentioning the flag and other equipment for Lloyd's expedition.

That fall, Arthur Aten, an Alaskan outfitter, and Merl LaVoy, a professional photographer and adventurer, began boating over a ton of food and gear closer to the mountain for their partners Browne and Parker. In the wake of Lloyd's disputed success on the mountain, the Fairbanks press had already been deriding the Professor's "Egghead" expedition for being overloaded with gear. Still, Parker and Browne sought out Lloyd's advice about his route, and obtained a photograph of his crux Northeast Ridge.

On February 1, 1912, following Aten and LaVoy's lead, Parker and Belmore Browne mushed out of the coastal town of Seward, hitching rides with mail carriers on dogsleds pulling light loads. They met Aten and LaVoy, moved up to the Chulitna River cache, then began mushing their huge loads around the mountain. Unaware of the routes taken by Cook or other Alaskan pioneers, they climbed an out-of-the-way, steep pass, before reaching a second pass with a straight-forward crossing over the Alaska Range. Initially elated about their "discovery" of this second pass, they later learned that "the Swede" had discovered and repeatedly used this crossing—Anderson Pass—years earlier.

Even though they had arrived in April when the Sourdoughs had blitzed the mountain, the winter winds roaring down the Muldrow Glacier forced them to delay, retreat to Kantishna, and resupply. While resupplying with sugar and other staples, Parker had the good fortune to chat with McGonagall, who characteristically told the Cheechako next to nothing about what to expect on the climb. Then the *News Miner* ran a story that made the Cheechakos sound desperate for food, but Browne had hunted big game all of his life. As temperatures gradually warmed in May, they hoofed it the three dozen miles up over McGonagall Pass and onto the Muldrow Glacier.

By early June, using ice axes instead of alpenstocks, pike poles, or hatchets, they began chopping steps up Lloyd's difficult Northeast Ridge. In addition to the slower yet traditional step-chopping techniques, they wore the same old-fashioned Appalachian Mountain Club creepers that Cook had lost before his 1906 climb.

Browne had to chop off the steep ridge crest in places to make room for their feet. They called the work "heartbreaking": constantly breaking trail in newly fallen snow and chopping steps. Where Parker dared to stop on the avalanche-prone slope to check its steepness with an inclinometer, it measured fifty degrees, dropping off even steeper several yards below. At thirteen thousand feet on this ridge, only halfway up the mountain in late spring, their thermometer registered twenty-six degrees below zero.

Everything the neophytic Sourdoughs claimed to quickly knock off two years earlier felt like desperate slow going to these experienced alpinists, despite warmer spring conditions. Slopes that looked several hundred feet away were actually several thousand feet higher. They contracted snow blindness. Their lips and noses were swollen, like their hands, which were cracked and stained with blood. Even worse, their greasy, fat-laced pemmican diet made them sick to their stomachs.

Above the ridge, avoiding a Sourdough-styled sprint, they established two more camps. From their 16,500-foot camp, Parker's team made two attempts on the higher South Summit. LaVoy, equipped by the National Geographic Society with the latest three-by-five-inch Graflex camera, documented their climb. And all three of them searched with field glasses for sign of the Sourdoughs' passage on the North Peak.

"Every rock and snow slope of that approach had come into the field of our powerful binoculars," Belmore Browne wrote in his oddly titled book *The Conquest of Mount McKinley*, duplicating the title of Dr. Cook's unbelievable 1907 *Harper's Magazine* article. "We not only saw no sign of a flagpole but it is our concerted opinion that the Northern Peak is more inaccessible than its higher sister." During their last and third attempt to climb the peak, while ponderously step-chopping, a fierce storm forced them back within three hundred feet of the South Summit.

Off the mountain a week later, camped on the tundra below the glaciers, a catastrophic earthquake knocked them off their feet. What shocked Browne, while perched on what he thought of as the rock-solid planet, was that it felt more like quivering jelly. Next to their tent, a thousand-pound boulder eerily drove across the tundra, gouging up earth; a nearby tundra pond boiled with the shock waves as if cooking; a muffled crash arose as the hill in front of them slid into the creek.

"The mossy surfaces of the hills were opening all about us," Browne wrote, "and as the surface opened the cracks filled with liquid mud and then suddenly everything was still."

They laughed to relieve the tension, then nervously dug for their tobacco. Up above them the Alaska Range had filled with a haze of avalanche dust.

Then, six miles away, the summit of the 11,890-foot-high, pyramidal Mt. Brooks exploded along with a six-mile-wide wall of adjoining peaks down onto the Muldrow Glacier, sending up a mountainous cloud; they battened down their tent and dove in as the tempest arrived. When they emerged, the once green plain of tundra was blanketed in ice crystals.

"There is no doubt that we would have all been killed if we had been on the mountain," said Parker.

In Kantishna, now emaciated from their efforts, they met McGonagall at a roadhouse, and then Anderson at his cabin at Glacier City, who served them tea, sourdough pancakes, and salmon. Browne, obviously impressed, referred to the miners as "sun-bronzed Sourdoughs." Then Anderson helped them find a leaky poling boat abandoned on Moose Creek, which they caulked—like Yako—for their float back out to civilization. On the Bearpaw River, upstream of the Tanana, they stopped and chatted for hours with Taylor.

Later, Taylor told a Fairbanks reporter that if Parker and Browne had made it to the top, they would've found the flag-pole. Although they didn't see it, they couldn't help being swayed by the generosity, strength, and knowledge of the 1910 climbers.

While ridiculed by the Fairbanks press about their seven-month-long, sea-level-to-twenty-thousand-foot epic, Parker and Browne had only kind things to say about Alaskans. During their journey home to the east coast, while meeting the press, they stopped criticizing the 1910 climbers. In *Conquest*, Browne wrote: "The more you see of the Alaskan prospector, the more you admire his breed, for these men pay a thousand-fold more in toil and suffering than the treasures that they win are worth."

As an intriguing red herring, Browne offered up a final opinion on the Sourdough mystery: "The lack of photographic evidence added to the contradictory statements [of Lloyd] made concerning this climb," he wrote, "make it a difficult matter for an outsider to tell much about it."

—◆—

Next year, in the final stage of the race to finish off Denali, the Karstens–Stuck expedition wisely carried and learned how to use their camera. In preparation for the climb, they found a stout yet extremely light birch pole to use as a flagstaff, but they would forget to bring a flag. They also packed a heavy barometer, a boiling point thermometer, and another accurate, minimum-register thermometer that Stuck left at fifteen thousand feet (recovered nineteen years later, it read −100°F).

While Archdeacon Stuck's duties as a traveling Episcopalian throughout Alaska had schooled him in wilderness life, among laconic pioneers of the North like Harry Karstens, Stuck's prickly erudition made him awkward company. A biographer wrote that his "life is the story of a very difficult, temperamental, exasperating, somewhat egocentric man." For a half dozen years, Stuck pestered Karstens with an invitation to lead the team. Karstens didn't mention that he was stalling because he wanted to go with Charles Sheldon instead. While waiting for an answer, Stuck asked the affable Sourdough Billy Taylor. But Taylor, fed up with being stiffed by Lloyd on the last climb, asked for a guaranteed five thousand dollars, which Stuck couldn't afford.

After Karstens finally joined the team, Stuck insisted on an expedition-style climbing strategy, rather than the alpine-style dash of the Sourdoughs. Stuck's plan to lay siege to the mountain followed the tradition of other Victorian-age explorers like the Italian Duke of Abruzzi, who had recently climbed Alaska's second highest peak, Mt. St. Elias. Stuck emulated the Duke, who hired American porters and Italian nobleman to carry his iron bedposts. (Stocking camps and slowly yo-yoing up and down a big mountain would continue to define high-altitude ascents for the next half century—testimony of how unorthodox and disputed the speedy Sourdough climb had been.)

Stuck described his game plan: "To roam over glaciers and scramble up peaks free and untrammeled is mountaineering in the Alps. Put a forty-pound pack on a man's back with the knowledge that tomorrow he must go down for another, and you have mountaineering in Alaska."

If Karstens had been calling the shots, the team would have mimicked the rapid-style 1910 attempt. Which would have pushed the older and unfit Stuck over the edge.

Most Alaskans knew Stuck acted as the titular leader, while the trail-savvy Karstens effectively led the team. From Stuck's point of view, Karstens was a working-class, semi-illiterate with a "juvenile keenness." But short of hiring Taylor, Anderson, or McGonagall—Stuck (forty-nine) figured that Karstens (thirty-three) was the only qualified man left in Alaska who could get him up Denali.

Like most Alaskan pioneers, Karstens fled north to pursue his dream of striking it rich in the Klondike gold rush. Instead, panning out only miniscule yellow flakes with McGonagall on the Seventy Mile River in eastern Alaska, they found their salvation running dogsleds, delivering mail in the hinterlands, and guiding wealthy hunters. Karstens—a decade younger than McGonagall, who claimed to name him the Seventy-Mile Kid—had stamina, an unerring touch with dogs, and intuitive winter survival techniques. He saved the older musher once from freezing to death and continued to look after McGonagall for most of his life. They became tight partners.

Karstens's most famous client had been Charles Sheldon. He described the Seventy-Mile Kid as "a tall, stalwart man, well-poised, frank, and strictly honorable, and peculiarly fitted by youth and experience for explorations in little-known regions." While lobbying with Belmore Browne in DC for the national park that would surround the mountain, the influential Sheldon was already making plans for Karstens to become its first Superintendent.

Stuck, Karstens, and their teammates Robert Tatum and Walter Harper spent eleven days mushing from Nenana, outside Fairbanks, into Kantishna. As soon as they met and consulted with Pete Anderson, Karstens began adding heelpieces to their lackluster four-point creepers in mimicry of the 1910 team's creepers. They even searched Lloyd's camp in hopes of finding his abandoned nine-point creepers. While Anderson shared the details of his climb, Stuck wrote in his diary, "Karstens believes him and I do too, though the task of carrying a 14 ft pole up that mountain must have been enormous and the feat sounds incredible."

Then they found Karstens's crony McGonagall, who wouldn't let them leave for the mountain until he searched the mining camps and found them looser-fitting moccasins—lest they freeze their toes like Anderson. Before they were on their way, McGonagall gave them a jar of his sourdough starter, which they carried to the base of the mountain, baking bread until the gangly Tatum spilled it all in their tent and earned his sobriquet, "The Sourdough Kid."

By the end of March they had hauled supplies over the McKinley River to their four-thousand-foot basecamp. Here, alongside the Clearwater River—an unusually translucent, spring-fed stream among the milk-colored glacial torrents draining the Alaska Range—the two leaders had already begun bickering. Stuck could be arrogant, while Karstens had an explosive temper.

Stuck's best contribution to the team may have been inviting the twenty-year-old Athapaskan Harper, an unflappable optimist, who had a great sense of humor and proved indefatigable. Stuck also brought along the minister in training, Tatum, twenty-one, who was timid and prone to crying jags. The imperious Stuck would describe Tatum in his diary as "a strange mixture of pluck & effeminency [sic], of cowardice & courage."

Karstens couldn't believe how "green" half of his team appeared. While Tatum and Harper wouldn't carry bedposts up the mountain like Stuck's Italian Duke hero, the Archdeacon made "the boys" fix him tea and cater to his whims.

The Archdeacon had a reputation for giving baptisms and providing Bible "instructions" throughout remote Alaskan villages. During his rounds by dogsled or on motor launches, he adopted boys and took them with him to prepare his camp and tend to chores that would free him up for journal keeping and prayer services. As an Englishman, Stuck had been raised on the Victorian, colonialist model of traveling with coolies or servants. Still, he held a righteous, if not contradictory, indignation about whites abusing native Alaskans. Whether through generous paternal spirit or lust, he spent months with these boys away from their homes, and then arranged scholarships for those he deemed fit to send away to boarding schools.

The misogynistic Archdeacon never married. Obviously smitten with Harper, Stuck traveled with the young man for two full years. Stuck even revealed his temptations while describing his charge: "clean-limbed, smooth-skinned, slender, and supple," he wrote in *Ten Thousand Miles with a Dogsled*, "his Indian blood showing chiefly in a slight swarth of complexion and aquilinity of feature." Elsewhere, his book overflows with mention of various boys and how "attractive" or "bright" they were.

Concerned that he would disgrace the church as a latent and celibate homosexual or a pedophile, after Stuck's death, Episcopalian superiors tried to bury or even burn his papers. His journal entries about Harper show why: "It is interesting and pleasing to see how the boy blossoms under affection," Stuck wrote. "I have not been so happy since the early days of my love for Edgar." Or a month later: "Although I rose at 4 a.m. and started a fire I was very glad to creep into bed again and snuggle up against Walter."

As the antithesis to Stuck, Karstens was a self-made, plainspoken American frontiersman with canted eyes and handsome broad cheekbones. The narrow-faced Stuck—sporting a jaunty-looking driver's cap on the trail—was fond of pretentious, grammatically correct pronouncements, concluded by smug, closemouthed smiles. Out on the trail Karstens quickly grew disgusted by Stuck's "sanctimonious-ness" and couldn't stand to watch him treating Harper and

Tatum as vassals. Even worse, Stuck whined, abstained from camp chores, and made his boys cook for him and pack and unpack his gear every day.

If Karstens suspected Stuck was a homosexual with an appetite for boys, he never mentioned it in his writings. But the wily Archdeacon—who taught school in Texas and worked on a ranch before joining the priesthood—had learned how to conceal his proclivities among heterosexual men. If Karstens had caught Stuck taking sexual advantage of Harper or Tatum, if such a dalliance had even occurred, there would have been hell to pay.

In correspondence to Charles Sheldon after the trip, Karstens called "the deacon" an "absolute Paresite [*sic*] & liar," neglecting to cook as he had promised, misrepresenting his mountaineering skills, and stealing all the glory of the climb for himself by writing and lecturing about Karstens as if he were a hired hand.

Karstens instead came to rely on Harper as a tireless trail-breaker, expert hunter, and all-around winter outdoorsman—the key skills needed for early Denali climbs. With two other sixteen-year-old "Indian boys" who accompanied them to the bottom of the mountain, they chased down and shot three caribou and a Dall sheep. They stripped away the fur and pared off the leanest meat rather than the fatty cuts that had sickened Browne's team (high altitude compromises digestion of fats and proteins). Then they boiled the sheep and caribou and shaped the meat into two hundred calorie-packed, fist-sized balls. They would never grow tired of eating this pemmican. Animal skins became their sleeping pads.

Throughout the blistering cold of April, Karstens wasn't just lured by Stuck's promise of fame and fortune. He knew that reaching the summit would likely garner him the respect to earn the coveted job through Sheldon as first superintendent of the soon-to-be created park surrounding the mountain.

Karstens took charge of freighting supplies over McGonagall Pass and down onto the Muldrow Glacier. The two stronger men were already helping the slow-moving Archdeacon with the aid of six dogs and two small sleds. Halfway up the Muldrow, Stuck or Karstens dropped a match and started a fire that destroyed some of their food and a lot of their clothing. While Stuck thought they were ruined, Karstens counseled calm, then began sewing a new tent and mittens and socks or delegating repair tasks as they continued up the mountain. Most expeditions would have turned around after such a setback.

By this point, Karstens had pulled Stuck aside and tried to shame him into doing his share of the work. He told Stuck to "quit his whining and get in and help himself we where [sic] out roughing it not at a 1st class hotel he promised to do better but he forgot all about it the second day."

During storms, they bided their time in canvas tents heated by woodstoves. For up to six hours a day, while Karstens puttered restlessly around camp, continuing to work on the creepers, Stuck tutored Harper with a library of physics, math, geology, and English books—a far cry from the light outfit and single magazine of the 1910 Sourdoughs.

In many ways, the conflict in this 1913 outing mirrored that of the rotund Lloyd and his lean teammates. This would be reenacted in many future Denali climbs, if only because mountaineering expeditions can be stressful, subzero, dangerous affairs. Every day, for weeks on end, you rope into, belay up, wait in the cold for, break the trail for, cook for, clean up after, and sleep next to flatulent and snoring partners. After a month, you're ready to kill if a teammate so much as spits, burps, or tells the same old joke just one more time. Clashing personalities and confrontations comprise the fabric of most climbing expeditions—particularly among teams of poorly matched dilettantes and experts.

At the crux ridge that Stuck would name after Karstens (rather than Anderson, Taylor, or McGonagall), they all grew even more anxious. The previous year's earthquake had shattered the ridge into a maze of ice blocks and rubble and crevasses. Harper and the Seventy-Mile Kid then spent twenty-one grueling days chopping steps up the mile-long spine, now a chaos of twisted ice, balancing in haphazard, precariously perched pedestals and towers. Karstens wrote to Sheldon that "2 blows of my axe sent one as big as a 2 storey [*sic*] house crashing and roaring into the basin thousands of feet below."

As a client who had been guided up Mt. Rainier and smaller peaks in Canada, Stuck knew that alpenstocks or the pike poles used by the 1910 climbers were hopelessly antiquated. So in Fairbanks before the trip he had a blacksmith make the four pair of inferior creepers, along with four-foot-long hickory and steel ice axes.

Although the ice axe's cutting properties may be taken for granted today, the 1913 team's ice axes were forged with straight adzes opposite the picks—curved adzes jammed in the snow. Still, it took the arms of a lumberjack to wield these seven-pound, three-ounce axes all day, making ice chips fly just for the sake of secure footing for the tottering deacon (during a 2013 Muldrow Glacier climb to the summit, Karstens's great grandson accompanied Harper's great nephew carrying an exact replica of the 1913 ice ax, cursing its weight most every day).

Since the Seventy-Mile Kid and Harper had not used ice axes before, they didn't complain about the weight. Still, unlike the awkward shovels or horizontally swung wood-chopping hand hatchets used by the Sourdoughs, these long axes could be more naturally swung straight up and down on a vertical parabola. They learned that with such a heavy steel head, the ax—often lifted with two arms and an accompanying grunt—could be swung up above the next footstep. Then, using gravity, the weight of the dropping adze did most of the chopping work.

Based on Stuck's experience being towed up mountains with alpine guides, he made the inexperienced mountaineers Karstens and Harper chop steps up most of the route—partly because of their jury-rigged creepers, which Stuck described as "terribly heavy, clumsy rat trap affairs" that they wouldn't don until they climbed above sixteen thousand feet.

Finally, Karstens could be seen waving at the ridge top and the way above was clear. The Archdeacon and his "postulant for the holy orders" Tatum climbed the veritable staircase to its top, beneath a three-hundred-foot-high tower of burnished, russet granite called Browne's Tower. The team then made three more camps on the Harper Glacier (named by Walter for his father).

Harper's journal showed him as thoughtful, emotive, even exuberant. He described their happiness for good weather days, the hard work of chopping steps, how "low" they felt prior to the summit, or the "wonderful transformation" of being on green, living tundra after the sterile, white, and blinding glaciers. On June 3, during a rest stop below sixteen thousand feet while moving camp up the Harper Glacier, they were discussing Lloyd's climb when Walter suddenly cried out, "I see the flagstaff!"

Robert Tatum wrote in his diary about their discovery of the pole (which many still don't believe): "Then Mr. K saw it and with the glasses the four of us saw it." Still, none of them described the steep, direct route that would have allowed the Sourdoughs to plant the pole on the ridge.

By the time they reached their 17,500-foot-high camp they had created a slow-moving record: 48 days on the mountain. Unlike the Sourdoughs, they should have been superbly acclimatized from all of the time spent up high, but the cold and fumes from their primus cooking stove trapped in the tent sickened them.

Everyone had trouble keeping their feet warm. For three days they scarcely wrote in their journals.

This high on the subzero, wind-blasted mountain, most climbers are anxiously looking over their shoulders for ominous signs—avalanches, cache-raiding ravens, lenticular clouds, or wind-driven banners of snow—while losing weight and nursing their frost-numbed bodies. The trick at these subhuman elevations is to get to the top, then descend as quickly as possible. But for generations to come, only those few climbers who have taken the trouble to hack and kick their way up the seldom-climbed Karstens Ridge could understand the magnitude of the Sourdough accomplishment. Stuck and company merely had to march for several hours up gentler slopes, due south from their 17,500-foot camp toward the higher south summit.

On the opposite mountain flank, across the shadowed basin north of their camp reared the infamous steep gully. The bottom of this chute was ominously littered with mounds of avalanche snow debris. A gaping, crevasse-cavern called a bergschrund showed the Harper Glacier pulling away from the steep, upper mountain. The gully above this moat is held between walls of solid granite and fractured shale, regularly peeling off in fusillades and cratering the snow. Depending on the time of year, the snow blows off or melts into glimmering, cement-hard ice that old-fashioned pike pole hooks and creepers—unless well sharpened—would barely dent. As steep as 55 degrees, climbing from 16,500 feet to 18,400 feet before attaining semi-level ledges and a curving ridge crest, the gully called the Sourdough Couloir had somehow, allegedly, been mastered by the 1910 climbers.

For the next half century, this forbidding, tilted architecture of rock and ice didn't entice anyone—panting from the lack of oxygen, bowed under heavy packs—who walked underneath it. Since no one in Karstens's party, nor Browne's, could imagine that their predecessors had climbed such a route, they figured that if the Sourdoughs summited, they had found a way to "march" around to it from Denali Pass rather than tackling it directly by the gully.

While slogging up the twenty-degree slopes across the way, on Stuck's breathless summit day of June 7, 1913, even the stoic Seventy-Mile Kid felt compelled to express his pain. "I had one of the most severe headaches [he wrote, continuing on successive pages in the tiny journal]: if it were not the final climb I should have stayed in camp but . . . . I managed to pull through. I put Walter in lead an [sic] kept him there all day with never a change. I took 2nd place on the rope so I could direct Walter and he worked all day without a murmur."

The summit day made Karstens expend more pencil lead than any other day in a diary no bigger than his palm. Taciturn, businesslike, and not built to celebrate, he so far forgot himself to write under that day's date: "'Hurrah' The south summit of Mt. McKinley has been conquered." Karstens told a reporter several years after the climb that he had carried the Archdeacon on his back to the summit. But the only one capable of such a feat that day would've been Harper, chopping all the steps and relieving Stuck from carrying the heavy barometer over his shoulder. (After the climb, the Archdeacon confessed in his journal, but not his book, about being piggybacked by Harper across the flooding McKinley River, while Karstens rescued Tatum from being drowned.) Stomping their feet down with less-than-ideal creepers, they zigzagged up slowly—just as Browne's team did the previous year. Since the weather held, even the gasping Archdeacon wouldn't stop them from topping out.

In his book Stuck did cop to falling down breathless once he reached the highest point in North America. When he came to, the Archdeacon gathered everyone together to pray. Karstens took several photographs, repeatedly showing Mt. Foraker, which, on their ascent route, could only be seen from the top. So no one would think to dispute their claim to the summit.

Following the 1910 Sourdough lead, Harper rammed their six-foot pole into the highest point, and attached a small American flag—since they'd forgotten to bring one, Tatum had sewn together and colored several handkerchiefs with stars and stripes. Karstens photographed it. Somehow, at seven degrees in a stiff north wind, they managed to spend an hour and a half on top.

—◦—

Stuck's mission, tending to indigent Native Americans throughout the North, was reflected in using the original name for the mountain, which would get renamed Mt. McKinley three years after his book *The Ascent of Denali* went to press.

No one would forget that the young native Walter Harper became first to stand atop the highest summit. Tena elders believed that Harper, like all Athapaskan people, carried the blood of Yako, creator of the mountain.

The Archdeacon usually honored native traditions. But unlike Cook, Dunn, or Wickersham, he didn't share the Denali creation story in his book. As a man of the cloth, it would have been heretical for Stuck to describe an alternate Creator. Nor did his teammates mention the ubiquitous raven in their diaries during their climb.

A modern reader might judge *The Ascent* to be as overwrought as Cook's book. The haughty Archdeacon took it one step further in the narrative and referred to himself in the third person (he worked with the famous Max Perkins at Scribner's, who also discovered and edited Ernest Hemingway, F. Scott Fitzgerald, and Thomas Wolfe).

Judging from his writing, Stuck underwent a transformation that Cook and Lloyd missed out on. Two months before being hauled to the summit, down at tree line, Stuck glared self-importantly into the camera. After reaching the top, he learned that the climb was a dream come true, because "a privileged communion with the high places of the earth had been granted." Like many Denali climbers deeply in over their heads, Stuck had found humility, which begs the question of how the Sourdoughs felt on their infinitely more challenging summit day, above a mind-boggling gully climb and a void never before walked across.

Contemptuously taking a dig at Lloyd and company, Stuck wrote, "I'd rather climb this mountain than discover the richest gold mine in Alaska." Still, in his book he called Anderson and Taylor "two of the strongest men, physically, in all the North." His coleader Karstens, a lot more qualified to judge the duo, praised Taylor for being strong and well trained, while Anderson, Karstens said, had an "exceptional ability to travel long distances without becoming tired." In his book, the Archdeacon also attempted, for the first time in history, to lay to rest which 1910 climbers did what.

"Lloyd himself reached neither summit," Stuck wrote. "As for the men who accomplished the astonishing feat of climbing the North Peak, in one almost superhuman march from the saddle of the Northeast Ridge, could most certainly have climbed the South Peak too" ("march" shows that Stuck had ruled out the gully as their climbing route). Later, Anderson or Taylor—either too nonchalant, laconic, or deceitful to give any details about the steep gully—told Stuck that they were greatly disappointed that they couldn't see the flagstaff from the Muldrow Glacier.

Even up high on the mountain, Stuck wasn't sure he could see their flagstaff with the naked eye, although he wrote in his book that: "through the field-glasses it was plain and prominent and unmistakable."

During a Congressional hearing on the issue of frauds and renaming the mountain shortly after the 1913 climb, a Philadelphia lawyer and champion of Cook testified:

Lloyd denies Cook. Browne denies Cook and Lloyd. Stuck denies Cook and Lloyd, and while not denying Browne, repeats over and over that Browne did not reach the top. There is a perfect epidemic of denials. So much so that it would be more accurate to nickname the peak Mount Denial instead of Mount Denali!

After this and a barrage of press about their climb, Stuck complained in letters to the angry Karstens that reporters got the facts wrong and lionized the Archdeacon with no mention of his companions. Although Stuck kept his word and shared half the profits from the *Scribner Magazine* article and book sales (Karstens later said this totaled around $1,500—a significant chunk of change for its day) he never forgave "the deacon," despite Stuck's attempts at reconciliation.

Word traveled quickly about Stuck and Karstens's climb and their sighting of the flagpole, which, for many, removed the veil from the disputed Sourdough North Peak climb. Billy Taylor sent Stuck a telegram on June 20: "Accept my sincere congratulations on successful ascent and thanks for confirming existence of our flagpole."

E.W. Griffin took the opportunity to place another ad in the *News Miner* for his mercantile store:

THE GRIFFIN FLAG STILL FLIES FROM THE SUMMIT OF MT. McKINLEY! SO REPORTS THE ARCHDEACON STUCK PARTY.

Stuck and Karstens's climb had been forged upon the Sourdoughs' success, with yet another unfit leader usurping the credit from more capable teammates. But the two parties' climbing styles couldn't have been more different. While the 1910 climbers claimed to have boldly sprinted up the mountain in winter conditions, the 1912 and 1913 climbers conservatively sieged the mountain in summer as if on a military campaign.

As for Karstens, no interviewer recorded why he climbed Denali, but his family, on down to a great grandson, believe that in addition to seeking a job with the new park, Karstens went in order to salvage McGonagall's reputation and take care of his friend. In other words, if the Seventy-Mile Kid could spot the flagpole that his old-timer partner lugged up—the flagpole that the Egghead expedition couldn't find with all their highfalutin cameras and field glasses—the nosy newspapermen and Cheechako doubters of the world would stop impugning his friend's honesty. The *Fairbanks Times*, while removing Lloyd's name from the summit party, oddly didn't even mention McGonagall.

In his 1914 book, Stuck—after he consulted Anderson and Taylor—explained McGonagall's role. Stuck praised him for discovering the namesake pass and stated that he also deserved "the credit of climbing some nineteen thousand five hundred feet, or to within five hundred feet of the North Peak." But the peak itself, he said, belonged only to Taylor and Anderson.

Over the next few years, the clouds darkening Lloyd's summit claim continued to lower. But the *News Miner*, along with his many Alaskan friends, clung to his story.

Like Dr. Frederick Cook and other frauds on Denali, Lloyd's life exemplified a more universal theme on how and why people lie. Lloyd had done it all of his life. This time, the lies, like the mountain, reached insurmountable proportions. His tale of climbing above eleven thousand feet and reaching both summits started out as simple northern-style, backslapping, beer-drinking exaggerations. Eventually pressured by those sponsors who banked and believed in him (or in Cook's case, by mounting debts and a burning desire for fame), the lies became a means to an end. In the minds of those haunted by unattainable dreams, lying often becomes indistinguishable from truth telling. Much easier, Lloyd figured in his final years of dipsomania and infidelities, to swallow a good story rather than the sword of his own failure. His Pioneer supporters—if not in it for their own gain and the irresistible opiate lie—drew a mantle of compassion around their otherwise good-natured friend and booster of all things Alaska.

Unlike Cook, Lloyd couldn't or didn't want to leverage his mountaineering fame into a money-making lecture tour, even though he had spoken briefly to several audiences in Fairbanks and Salt Lake City. Over the next three years, Alaskan newspapers in Juneau and Fairbanks promoted his fame as the conqueror of McKinley and reported his potential to become a millionaire, shipping out boatloads of antimony ore from Kantishna and discovering other rich ledges. Judge James Wickersham had already expressed skepticism in his diary about Lloyd's honesty after they invested in a worthless mine together. Still, in an effort to enlarge all things Alaska, including Lloyd, Wickersham penned a lengthy tribute to Lloyd's climb in the *Washington Times*—a story he would regret in later years as it became obvious that Lloyd was lying. Lloyd repaid the favor and remained an active Republican delegate supporting the budding territory's congressional representative, Wickersham, while traveling to Juneau and outside the state to cast his vote and promote the party. (The popular Wickersham, as it turned out, is the only politician whose name is still attached to the mountain.)

Lloyd spent the last year of his life suffering from liver and heart ailments, joined in Fairbanks by his recently married son, Reese. (Mildred Lloyd Murry would believe that her "Grandpa Lloyd" got seriously ill on the Muldrow Glacier and that "this is the reason he made up part of the story.") Shortly after Lloyd's admittance to the St. Joseph's Hospital in Fairbanks on July 17, 1916, while chatting up a nurse, he died suddenly and unexpectedly of a stroke in front of his dinner tray.

"One of the most widely known men in Alaska," the *News Miner* eulogized, praising him for his patriotism and leadership in planting "Old Glory on top of the world."

Hundreds of friends came to Lloyd's funeral, braving a heavy downpour. Even if it had been a clear day, buildings blocked the view of Denali from the gravesite. Both Cheechakos and Pioneers, according to the newspaper, attended. The pallbearers included Bill McPhee, now losing his eyesight (his saloon would close down the next year amid the oncoming Prohibition). Noticeably absent were the Swede, Billy, and Charlie—they had already carried Lloyd for too long to get wet in the rain that day.

───◆───

Their story influenced climbers around the world. Still, modern climbers—now schooled in fast, alpine-style climbing—began to rethink the impossibly speedy Sourdoughs and their Sisyphean feat in heaving the flagpole up the dangerous Karstens Ridge and the final, steep gully. Something just didn't fit.

The similarities to Cook—widely dismissed for his summit claim by Denali climbers over the last century—are startling. Neither Cook nor Lloyd's boys knew how to read their barometer (which would've established their high-point elevations). Both Cook and Lloyd vaunted about summit flags unseen by others. Both returned without pictures from the top during speedy climbs up unlikely, steep, seldom-repeated routes (two Russians recently summited via the circuitous route Cook supposedly took, circling up from the south to the northeastern Karstens Ridge). Finally, both parties lacked mountaineering experience and both signed affidavits.

Lloyd clearly didn't join the summit party, but the other three Sourdoughs—if any of them did actually reach the North Peak—lied by signing the affidavit about reaching the higher south summit. So the credibility of all four climbers remains suspect.

While digging for and recovering the missing flagpole or other left-behind pieces could resolve the mystery, this excavation—at high altitude along steep inaccessible terrain on an exposed ridge—would be an expedition in itself. Then, if the flagpole or guylines or signboard can't be found, it would prove nothing.

Yet, by digging deeper into the climbing annals of Denali—examining its history along with its early photographs, and what little is known about the three reticent Sourdoughs—other small truths might be uncovered. Starting with the historic context, from present to past, the Sourdough accomplishment can be put in perspective through more accomplished climbers' experience on the same route.

In 2016, Brian Okonek, one of the mountain's foremost experts, studied the early climbs and couldn't understand how the Sourdoughs climbed the route so quickly. Okonek thinks that the 1913 team believed that they saw the flagpole. But they may have instead glimpsed an iced-over rock wall—distorted by distance and shadows or their own high-altitude oxygen starvation—that resembled a flagstaff.

Another expert, the park service mountaineering ranger and Alaskan Mark Westman—who has climbed a record seven routes on Denali—believes that the Stuck–Karstens party pole sighting is a conspiracy of Alaskans incensed by Cheechako outsiders. Although it might seem to be a stretch for them to lie, they were proud northern pioneers. So, by validating the Sourdoughs' climb of the North Peak along with their 1913 climb on the South Summit, the Stuck–Karstens party would have ensured that Alaskans fully "owned" Denali. Following this logic, this 1913 pole sighting by an Alaskan team could also have been concocted to refute the outsider "Eggheads" in 1912, who claimed that they didn't see the flagpole.

In 1977, another team tried to reenact the 1910 climb. Sixty-seven years after the Sourdoughs, seven strong climbers took turns carrying a fourteen-foot spruce pole up over Anderson Pass and onto the Muldrow Glacier. The pole was awkward, the leader Jeff Babcock recalled, but not a burden to his large crew. Since they had cut the pole and dried it over the previous winter it wasn't as heavy as the sap-filled tree that the Sourdoughs cut down on their way up the mountain.

After two months of load-carrying, the well-acclimated Babcock and Andy Butcher left their eighteen-thousand-foot Harper Glacier camp on a pleasant May morning with two thermoses of hot drinks, packing energy bars instead of donuts, and strolled an hour down to the infamous couloir. They strapped on twelve-point crampons over bulbous-looking white Bunny Boots, invented by the military during the Korean War for subzero temperatures. Roped together, they began step-kicking, placing snow pickets that they clipped the rope into, and zigzagging up what they thought to be thirty- to forty-degree snow—an easy climb for an experienced Denali veteran like Babcock.

A third of the way up, black, softball-sized rocks started zinging past their heads. "Let's get the hell out of here," Babcock yelled. Thwarted, they speared the pole into rocks alongside the couloir and descended—booting back down the gully as quickly as they could. They returned to camp, humbled, ten hours after leaving. In half of the time taken by the Sourdoughs, they'd made one-tenth the altitude gain.

More ominously, the year before, another strong team had a completely different experience with the couloir while climbing the difficult Pioneer Ridge that paralleled Karstens Ridge. On July 12, 1976, the six-man team decided to split up. The stronger two, including the accomplished alpinist Steve Swenson—who was skeptical of the 1910 feat—climbed over the North Peak and down to Denali Pass on an easier route than the Sourdoughs' direct route.

Unbeknownst to Swenson and his partner, one of their four teammates behind contracted altitude illness. Since they needed to bring the staggering, sick climber down immediately, they started belaying one another down from the top of the Sourdough Couloir. Several hundred feet later, one of the climbers fell on the steeper ice at the top of the couloir, pulled out the belay anchor and all four plummeted 1,500 feet down to the Harper Glacier.

Two died immediately from massive head and chest trauma. Of the two survivors, Bill Joiner was knocked unconscious and hung upside down all night long in a cocoon of rope; Larry Fanning suffered two broken legs. With miraculous timing the next morning, some passing climbers, thinking at first (from a mile away) that the bodies were remains of a climber cache scavenged by ravens, eventually saw the four inert bodies and rushed up to save Joiner and Fanning.

Several days later, a military helicopter flew out all four victims. While Fanning refused to talk about the accident, Joiner lost all of his fingers to frostbite and has no memory of what caused the fall. Surprisingly, Joiner believes—if only for the sake of embracing the inspirational legend—that the Sourdoughs did in fact complete the climb.

In 1967, the mountain's greatest tragedy also occurred high on the Muldrow Glacier Route. A ferocious windstorm hit yet another splintered team and seven climbers were lost somewhere between the bottom of the Sourdough Couloir and the summit. Their bodies, mysteriously snowed over, were never recovered.

Then in 1954, a team of Alaskans who modeled their climb after the 1910 Sourdoughs, walked into the Ruth Glacier. They climbed the south buttress route (with a similar approach to Cook's claimed ascent), then reached the summit. To complete their magnificent traverse, they walked down the Harper Glacier to Karstens Ridge. Their leader, the park ranger Elton Thayer, took the rear position on the rope to safeguard his partners below. But on the steepest part of the ridge, he slipped, fell past his partners and pulled them several hundred feet down the mountain: Thayer was killed; Morton Wood broke his hip. The other two climbers, uninjured, slid Wood down to the Muldrow Glacier, made him comfortable in a tent, left him all of their food and trekked out for help. Several days later, a helicopter whisked him out to the hospital.

After the 1910–1913 climbs, the mountain remained untouched until 1932. That year, two expeditions started up the Muldrow Glacier. In late April, a park service team of four men succeeded in climbing both peaks of Denali. From the top of the North Peak, they looked down toward the Sourdough Couloir but saw no flagstaff. They had hoped to go looking "for a busted piece of the pole itself, or at least a piece of rope they used to guy it," said Grant Pearson, one of the climbers. As the next superintendent of the national park surrounding the mountain, he too would fall in line as a true believer, showing how most Alaskans depended upon this legend without factual verification. He referred to the Sourdough climb as "one of the greatest feats of mountain climbing ever accomplished." Since the ridge down to the top of the couloir looked difficult and would have taken hours of additional step-chopping, they elected to return by their ascent route. They crept back down low-angled snowfields toward Denali Pass, buffeted by a sudden storm.

"We left those relics of the expedition that started in McPhee's saloon for the next climbers," Pearson told his biographer years later. "So far as I know no one has ever found them."

During their descent in 1932, at eleven thousand feet on the Muldrow Glacier they found the tents from another expedition but no climbers. They had expected to meet its leader, Allen Carpé, who had been flown into six thousand feet on the glacier with four companions (three of whom waited down lower on the mountain) to measure cosmic light rays.

Another mile and a half down, they found the dead body of Carpé's companion, Theodore Koven, who had died from his injuries after climbing out of a crevasse. Stunned, they loaded the corpse into a sled, hauling with, instead of tying into their only climbing rope.

"I was snowshoeing along about fifty feet back on the sled," Pearson said, "with Harry right behind me, without warning, the snow fell away under my snowshoes. I plunged into sudden darkness."

Pearson had broken a crevasse bridge and fallen forty feet. Aside from biting through his lip and lacerating his face, he had no major injuries. After his teammates dropped him a rope, it took hours to extricate him because of the overhanging lip of the crevasse. Then they buried and marked Koven's body on the glacier and continued down—all carefully roped together.

While they found the crevasse that had trapped Carpé, there was no answer to their shouts. "I am still haunted by the thought of how Carpé must have felt," Pearson wrote, "if he survived the fall, lying there in the icy darkness slowly freezing to death."

In 1932, no one in North America had Carpé's glacier experience, rope skills, or technical climbing gifts. He had knocked off coveted first ascents on several of the continent's most difficult peaks but died in a crevasse fall on a gentle Muldrow Glacier slope a mile below the start of the real climbing. His and Koven's deaths on terrain that the rotund Lloyd had repeatedly traipsed across rendered the story of the 1910 climb and its members' survival even more far-fetched. Pearson wasn't the only one to wonder how the Sourdoughs made it through unroped and unscathed. In the *New York Times* article, even Lloyd had called the crevasses "terrible. . . . Most of them appear to be bottomless." (At least eight climbers have now died in crevasse falls on Denali.)

In 1937, a few more details about the Sourdough climb leaked out from an unlikely meeting in a roadhouse outside McKinley Park. In the midst of reading Stuck's *Denali* book, Seattle mountaineer Norman Bright looked up to see a balding man who looked like a portly, jovial plumber Bright knew in Fairbanks. The waitress told Bright that the book he was reading featured this man.

"How far up the mountain did you get?" Bright asked.

"To the top," the stranger said calmly.

Clearly, he didn't look like Karstens and couldn't have been one of that climber's partners because the other three 1913 climbers were either dead or down south.

He had the widest shoulders Bright had ever seen. Puzzled, forgetting about the 1910 Sourdoughs, Bright asked again for the man's name: it was Billy Taylor!

So Bright began interviewing the affable fifty-four-year-old, wheezing as he ran outside to feed his sled dogs, his false teeth clacking as they talked in the bunk room of the roadhouse. He wore huge bib overalls, a dirty, wrinkled shirt and a beat-up hat. He smelled like huskies but smiled like a gentleman.

Taylor had left Ottawa and lit out for the goldfields as a teenager after the death of his parents. He told Bright that Cook had definitely inspired them to make the climb.

Asked to describe Lloyd during the climb, Taylor replied, "He was probably close to sixty—well, in the fifties anyhow. I imagine he was damn close to sixty. He was awful fat. Had kind of a nervous breakdown [in 1916] and just keeled over."

"He was fine in his way," Taylor said generously, "but he was lookin' for too much fame. He conflicted his stories by telling his intimate friends he didn't climb it and told others he was at the top. We didn't get out till June and, then, they didn't believe any of us had climbed it. But Stuck verified the climb. He found the pole. The halfbreed [Harper] was the first one to see it."

"Lloyd was the head of the party and we never dreamed he wouldn't give a straight story," Taylor added, "I wish to God we 'hadda' been there [at Lloyd's newspaper interview]. Of course our intimate friends believed us."

His demeanor changed when asked to describe Peter Anderson: "Big husky Swede," Taylor said. "Hell of a good fellow on the trail. Him and I'd go along and never have no trouble at all. He was a husky 'sonofagun.' We done all the work but we never got credit for nothin'. None of those points was named after us," Taylor had been referring to Browne's Tower and the peaks above the Muldrow Glacier: Brooks, Tatum, and Carpé.

"I had implicit confidence in Lloyd," Taylor said, "so I never kept no data [diary] on it at all." Anderson, he said, worked as a tinsmith in the nearby town of Nenana, but was never home.

As for McGonagall, Taylor hadn't seen him for years. McGonagall had clearly been the odd man out on the Denali climb, an old-timer who kept his own company.

Taylor described their bacon and beans and caribou diet on the mountain as if they ate like kings. As for their diet on the eighteen-hour day, "Had doughnuts on the highest," he said. "That's all we took up with us—and hot chocolate—a thermos bottle apiece. Just took a half a dozen doughnuts in a sack and started out. I had three left when I got back."

He mentioned, not a little bit proud, how Stuck and Karstens spent nearly a month for what took Taylor and companions "one day, by God!

"Just breaking day, a little after three, when we started, and I know it was dark—getting dusk—when we got back. I know it was an even eighteen hours. I don't know the exact time. We never paid no attention to that.

"We took our climbing poles and creepers and walked right over everything and forgot about steps. Carried knapsacks, but we had nothing to pack but a little grub, thermos bottle, rope, candles, camera."

Strangely, while Taylor didn't chop steps, he said nothing about the steep Sourdough Couloir. He told Bright that where they didn't feel comfortable lugging the big pole over their shoulders, they dragged it with a line. His description of planting the flagpole matched Lloyd's to the inch (although he'd mildly dismissed his leader *balling up* the story, Taylor proudly kept a copy of that 1910 *New York Times* article in his cabin). He told Bright: "We dug down in the ice with a little ax we had and built a pyramid of 15 inches high and we dug down in the ice so the pole had a support of about 30 inches and it was held by four guy-lines—just cotton ropes."

Taylor then described to Bright the final ridge from the couloir top looking down the thirteen-thousand-foot Wickersham Wall as a knife blade, even steeper than Karstens Ridge.

"Why didn't you use climbing ropes?" Bright asked.

"Didn't need 'em," Taylor replied.

By now Bright had taken the Sourdough tale hook, line, and sinker. So he asked, "How did it feel to stand on the top of the highest mountain of North America and know the whole continent was beneath you?"

"Well, of course, the altitude made you feel light-like," Taylor replied. "You had to watch yourself or your feet would come up quick.

"That day we was up there," Taylor said about the summit, "it was thirty below. I know it was colder than hell. Mitts and everything was all ice."

When Bright asked why they didn't climb the higher South Peak, Taylor replied, "We set out to climb the North Peak. That's the toughest peak to climb—the North."

Hours later, verifying much of what Lloyd had included in the *New York Times* story about the lower mountain, the train to Fairbanks had pulled in and Taylor loaded his dogs on board.

Bright asked whether he'd climb the mountain again.

"Yes," replied Taylor, "if there was enough money in it. But not just for sport." As the train pulled out, he waved and shouted, "Goodbye Norman."

While these last words from a Sourdough would convince most other climbers, Bright (who had never been on the mountain) learned nothing about the steep couloir. Did they really muscle their way up this gully to the "knifeblade" without chopping steps? And then they had to get to the summit and back down—without ropes or belays—exhausted in subzero temperatures, on primitive creepers and hooked pike poles. It couldn't have been done solely through superhuman effort and luck; and since they were inexperienced, they lacked technique. If Taylor had been telling the truth, he'd left something out of his story.

In the scant years given to a habitual bachelor, he worked like a bear, digging and chopping in the played-out tunnels he carved and dynamited out of the hard rock underlying Denali.

A later superintendent, Fritz Nyberg, of the national park surrounding the mountain observed, "Bill Taylor was built like a packhorse, one of the toughest of them all."

Taylor found his own measure of success above and beyond his physical prowess as a miner. Five years after the climb, he became the Kantishna mining commissioner. In 1915, he left the North for the first time in eleven years, traveling to San Francisco and Seattle to promote Alaskan mining and find investors to help him remove ore from the remote, hard-to-reach lodes he prospected. But the railroad or road access he hoped for would not materialize in his lifetime.

Blue-eyed Billy was modest to a fault, gentle and kind to his horses and dogs. Since he'd been orphaned as a young teen, he had no schooling, but in the long dark that comprised life swallowed by the northern winters, he immersed himself in the ancient Greek legends for spiritual sustenance. An eternal optimist, even after his failed partnership with Lloyd on the mountain and in the mines, Taylor named his most promising silver and gold find for Damon, who offered his life for his soon to be executed friend Pythias—but unlike that hopeful friendship in which they saved one another's lives, Lloyd had completely betrayed Taylor. And Taylor's "Damon and Pythias Deposit" never panned out.

Lloyd, trying to make amends in his deceptive *New York Times* story, had said: "Taylor and me have been partners for years, and (I don't claim that is because of any good qualities of mine) I have never had words with him. He is, beyond question, one of the finest men you ever met."

Taylor fought hard for everything he earned. After a mining accident, he bore the stigma of losing one of his fingers; the newspapers reported his lengthy stays in the hospital for unnamed illnesses. Impoverished, like McGonagall and Anderson, he suffered unduly, yet never complained.

Still formidable in his late fifties, Taylor registered for the draft in 1942, two years before his death. Forced to leave his $25 tent home, he too died in the Fairbanks hospital, seven years after Norman Bright interviewed him. Overturning the usual bias of Fairbanks papers for its local heroes, the short obituary referred to his "widely disputed ascent of the mountain."

His partner Anderson, the indefatigable force of nature, had only one thing to say about the supposed 1910 achievement: "Better stick to mining." Still, after years of striking out, he could no longer abide life as an impoverished pick-and-shovel man working under martinets like Lloyd. He found a new life in Nenana, running up and down the Tanana River in his small motorboat, repairing stoves and other metal implements essential to life on the frontier. For a brief time, Fairbanks editors remembered his name and reported snippets of news: being deputized to root out an Indian attack (which turned out to be a prank) in Kantishna, getting shot at while boating during the Tanana (they never caught the gunman), and ducking out of his own wedding to stake another mining claim (which never panned out).

His first marriage ended, mysteriously, with his wife's death. Never lacking female companionship, he remarried Marie Schnell, but seven short years later, she died from diabetes. Neither union brought him children.

While he lacked his teammate's Sampson shoulders, he stood several inches taller than five-foot-nine Taylor—making them both veritable giants for their time. (Latter day ecto-morph alpinists who perform alpine-style dashes rarely sport these formidable physiques, showing yet another chink in the

Sourdough claim.) Aside from Anderson's third marriage, at seventy-three, to Charlotte Bell, fifty, the details of his life and prodigious feats of strength have been forgotten. His once-towering form lies forgotten in a Sitka graveyard where the sea air has erased critical names and dates from the tombstones. With his common name amid a flood of Scandinavian immigrants at that time, and no surviving family, his death date remains a mystery.

With Anderson gone, reporters repeatedly pestered the more accessible, albeit snappy, McGonagall. A diminutive perfectionist who didn't suffer fools gladly, he finally held forth to the more scholarly mountaineers—such as the mapmaking scientist and Denali expert Brad Washburn or the climbing historian Francis Farquhar.

Born to Irish immigrants in Michigan, the younger McGonagall held a rugged, high-cheek-boned charisma, parting his hair down the middle. Unsuited for the strenuous labor of mining, he found no shortage of work pounding nails and policing rivers in and around Fairbanks. As he aged, he grew stooped and wore professorial wire-rim glasses. Despite his working-class roots, he often sported a suit and tie.

Norman Bright caught up to him in 1937, but didn't get far, aside from learning that McGonagall thought of Lloyd as "a good beer drinker and teller of tall stories." McGonagall added, cussedly about the climb, that he got "nothing out of it but a lot of hard work" and that he "didn't want to go in the first place."

Several years later, Farquhar had more luck with McGonagall in his tiny yet impeccable clapboard home in Fairbanks; until the end of his life, he worked and enjoyed a reputation as a craftsman carpenter. It didn't hurt that the

Seventy-Mile Kid, his old friend, sat in on the interview. Karstens, in fact, never heard McGonagall talk so much about the climb. "Billy and Pete were skookum," McGonagall told them, "and I was pretty good in those days. Lloyd was too old and too fat—he never got above 11,000 feet. The only reason we climbed the mountain was to prove Doc Cook hadn't done it and we could. By just looking at the mountain we knew he was a liar. We proved we climbed it by setting up the pole."

On a blue streak, he bragged that they could've climbed the South Peak too, if they knew it was higher, but they figured the pole wouldn't be seen there. As for why he didn't go to the top of the North Peak, he waved his hand and said, "Why should I? I'd finished my turn carrying the pole before we got there. Taylor and Pete finished the job—I sat down and rested, then went back to camp. Sure I could have gone up, but what for? The others had the pole and didn't need any help."

As if that wasn't enough, Farquhar (editor of the *American Alpine Journal*) would also accept the trio's alleged second ascent—a month after the first superhuman blitz of the mountain—as gospel. As Karstens listened in mute astonishment to this even more unbelievable feat, McGonagall stated that he, the Swede, and Billy returned to get pictures for Lloyd, going three days straight without stopping or pitching camp, from the tundra to 18,200 feet. "Until," as the *Fairbanks Times* erroneously reported, "there was no more mountain to climb."

Farquhar took all of this tallest tale as unadulterated fact, published it, and then the legend—thanks to him, Bright and Washburn—was born anew. If not entirely believed.

Epilogue: The Summit, 2016 and 1910

Despite the years behind me and the mountain above, I still felt strong yet wary that this would change as climbed higher. The usual summit-day paranoia. So I switched out of metronomic mode and started paying more attention. At least two of my young companions were moving slower, suffering from high-altitude headaches and nausea. Two thousand feet below, through a break in the clouds 14 miles away, Mt. Foraker, 17,400 feet, rose above a cresting, frozen riptide of seldom-climbed peaks.

Lift one foot above the other, pause a beat with the mountaineer rest step, breathe, and plunge in the ax, then repeat. Another hour crept by.

Here, on what used to be the most remote wilderness on the continent, we followed a trail of frozen footsteps. Compressed by the weight of hundreds of climbers, this fossilized-looking, dehydrated-orange-urine-stained snow path remains in place like a raised sidewalk even as the untrodden snow around it blows away. Come the next major storm all would be scoured away as if the mountain had never been defiled.

Every rope length, we passed thigh-high, green bamboo wands that bristled like mountain whiskers from the snow. Although not needed under the present mile-wide visibility, if the clouds dropped and put us into a depthless whiteout, these wands could save our lives by showing the way back down.

In case storm or injury demanded we stop and dig shelter, we carried shovels, stoves, pots, down bags, sleeping pads, radios, and down jackets. Still, most bivouacs this high on the mountain are invitations to frostbite or worse. I had never crossed this half-mile-wide plateau, understatedly called "the football field," without looking for or thinking about the seven men lost here in 1967. We could've been walking over their desiccated remains.

I remembered yet again my own past struggles here. In the winter of 1982, alone and abandoned by my teammates—who ran down, frightened that a storm would blow us to kingdom come—I repeatedly laid down, and then after each collapse, forced myself to stand and stumble on across this interminable flat football field, bubbly breathed from high-altitude pulmonary edema, unable to feel my toes.

But this day, to my surprise, I felt reserves of strength unlike any past visits to this death zone. We climbed the final, 40-degree headwall to the 20,100-foot summit ridge, plunging our axes in every other step. At a rest break, I shouted up congratulations for two acquaintances—briefly visible above—who had just finished climbing the infamous Cassin.

Then, suddenly as a cork popping from a shaken champagne bottle, we couldn't climb any further. We had reached the summit. I couldn't believe that I'd done it: my age and past high-altitude problems and fears of not coming home had nearly convinced me that I didn't have the right to try.

From previous visits, I knew that we stood on a colossal cornice with a dizzying view down the south face, but shifting clouds put us in and out of what appeared to be a featureless white room, alternating with patches of blue sky.

I knew this place for transcendent power and beauty. But months would pass before I could process this ascension, to identify why I repeatedly returned, or what I had learned.

My high-altitude mutant teammate Michael Hutchins pulled out a surprise ceremonial kata scarf from Nepal (he'd spent the previous winter teaching Sherpas how to climb) and as it caught the wind like a flag, he tied it around my neck. "Happy 60th!" Michael shouted. We all shook hands. I couldn't speak.

I felt elated for Hamilton, Cosker, and Inman, particularly since two of them were hurting, but had pressed on despite their high-altitude nausea. All three walked over and stood on the highest point. As for Hutchins, strolling about as if it were the beach, unaffected by the altitude, he could've done the climb in his sleep.

Before leaving, we had one last task, ritualistically performed by most climbers who preceded us here. It used to involve taking a bulky, several-pound camera out from under the jacket, removing the lens cap and cleaning fog off the viewfinder—alternately blowing on your wooden fingertips—until you could take a photograph. Since most teams carry more than one camera, if lenses or film were frozen, someone usually snags at least one blurry image for posterity. Fortunately, the once-popular ritual of planting poles and photographing flags on summits has long since been abandoned. When climate change fully melts the glaciers, hundreds of sub-fourteen-foot poles and tattered flags will emerge, littering the surrounding slope.

If the mountain or the route below us had never been climbed before, we would've taken a wide-angle photograph—showing recognizable topography below and behind the metal survey disc marking the summit—to prove that we made the ascent. Today, with multiple teams coming and going on this increasingly well-worn path to the belfry of North America, no one would argue that we hadn't rung the bell; even though I carefully, respectfully, stood several feet below the actual summit.

I lifted my wafer-thin, lanyarded iPhone out from under my neck, pulled my teammates into a scrum, and quickly removed a glove and held out an arm to snap a picture of our crowded-together faces. Like the Greek Hydra taking a selfie.

The time-honored ritual complete, I paid out rope and went last, windmilling my camera-taking arm to bring back circulation to my icy fingers. Hutchins and I both manned the rear positions on our two rope teams, ever vigilant in case we needed to "catch" our less-experienced, slow-moving partners. My knees ground audibly beneath the prosthetic hip as I braced the ax in case Sergeant Hamilton should slip in front of me, so I could stop the fall. I kept the rope tight, remembering Elton Thayer on Karstens Ridge, or four others who had fallen the length of the Sourdough Couloir across the way. Now, and hopefully for the last time, I had to make it down safely. We crawled along for hours on slopes I would have happily loped down unroped if I were alone.

Moving without belays over moderately steep mountains, quickly, was the path I missed more than anything from the halcyon days of my youth. To a non-climber this type of activity would be perceived as reckless, but I embraced it as a game of tight control and focused hyperawareness of my body movements and surroundings—like riding on a roadbike down a high pass without needing to squeeze the brakes.

Now, as a sexagenarian, descending from 18,400 feet down the awkwardly angled "Autobahn"—named after many high-speed and fatal crashes—I felt thankful for the fixed rope.

I kept my legs splayed to avoid catching my pants with a crampon spike. And I watched Hamilton's every move, just as Hutchins watched Cosker and Inman because stumbling footwork often precedes a fall. Even a ten-foot bouncing slide caught by the rope would be enough to catch crampons and snap lower leg bones. Over the years I had rescued three different victims off this slope.

We reached our 17,200-foot camp in a not-so-fast 12-hour round trip, but I could've walked or climbed all night. With my vivid memories of catching up to the team here and crawling frozen-footed into our tent in the winter of 1982, Ranger Tomato thoughtfully handed me a pouch of hot freeze-dried lasagna. I inhaled it, promptly fell asleep, and dreamed soundly as a teenager.

During the morning's descent, we walked down and around crowds clambering up the narrow crest of the west buttress, staggering under heavy packs and jostling to clip into the fixed ropes. I pretended to be the client that Ranger Tomato needed and let him show me his technique for shortened rope travel as if I had never coiled one before. He also reprimanded me about the summit day for removing a weaker team member's pack and leaving it temporarily clipped in below the final headwall. Yet Tomato, above the law, routinely skied around crevasses alone and unroped—an audacious safety infraction that would cost most rangers their jobs. Since expeditions are fraught with tension and hubristic personalities, I reassumed my role as a follower to avoid conflict.

The névé squeaked with each crampon spike's penetration, a dozen times with every pivoting footstep, as if I were tickling the ivories on a grand piano. Three vertical miles below shimmering tundra ponds—filled with algae, fish, and bugs and the sound of running water—felt whole worlds away. Where we lurched along on a monochromatic, permanently iced-over ridge of Denali, the only signs of life were transient climbers. We quickly flatfooted our way down the final headwall, protected—unlike the Sourdoughs—by fixed rope and state-of-the-art gear.

At our 14,300-foot medical camp I took off my shirt and stood mute under the hot sun, lost in rapture for the tawny granite buttresses above, capped by a plume of wind-driven snow flying off the summit plateau. I could almost feel the high-altitude rock warm under my fingertips, the reverberation of my ax crackling into ice, as past climbs merged into present and all my trips became one. For a brief moment, yet again, I felt like I belonged here. This was my mountain.

Opening my eyes, I knew that this would be my last Denali trip. I could never have it so complete again.

Then young Hutchins stepped out of his tent with a beatific smile. Wondering whether he felt the same as me, I asked whether he had taken the trouble after tying the kata around my neck to walk two feet higher and stand on the absolute highest point. "It never occurred to me," he replied, innocence lighting up his face.

"Why not?" I asked, and since I too had deliberately abstained from walking the last couple feet, I already knew his answer:

"Because that would've been conquest and that's not what we came here to do."

———

At dawn, the inevitable trouble arrived when a Japanese team on their way down from the summit radioed for help. A sixty-six-year-old man named Masayuki Ikeda had collapsed near Denali Pass, incapacitated by sudden blindness, unable to walk. He had contracted the rare high-altitude cerebral edema. With his brain swollen by fluids, on the verge of death, only immediate descent would save him.

In less than two hours, the stripped-down park service helicopter arrived from sea level with a "short-haul" cable and basket. Hovering above 18,400 feet, without the added weight of passengers to further compromise engine limitations at high altitude, the pilot lowered the basket from a cable. Ikeda's teammates strapped him in, now pulseless, and the helicopter lifted him off the ridge, penduluming him out over the void. If there had been turbulence or lack of engine power while carrying the now dangerously weighted basket, the pilot—unbeknownst to most victims riding these short-hauls—would've released the cable from the helicopter. Fortunately, the air remained still. Within minutes, the basket came swaying down through still air to our 14,300-foot camp beneath the copter like a spider on a strand. Ranger Tomato lifted Ikeda out of the basket and placed him gently inside the helicopter. Inman and Hamilton jumped aboard and the pilot lifted then banked the ship into an accelerating dive toward thicker, resuscitative air as our medics took turns performing chest compressions and breathing into their patient's lungs.

By mid-morning, warped from their efforts, they declared him dead there in the helicopter at seven thousand feet. This, the year's second climbing fatality, would comprise one of seventeen climbers whom rangers treated or rescued that summer under life-threatening circumstances (three days after Ikeda's death, the park service helicopter saved a climber who had collapsed at 17,200 feet with high-altitude pulmonary edema).

The next evening, exploiting the cold nighttime hours that froze dangerous crevasse bridges, we skied roped together down to the seven-thousand-foot ski plane landing strip and basecamp. From the summit we had dropped thirteen thousand feet—four thousand feet more than Everest's summit to basecamp.

Like bloodhounds after a scent, we hunted down a wand marking our cache of left-behind gear from three weeks earlier and dug up our lager and IPA. In a large tent, rejoining our medics, we toasted one another until the wee hours, happy to be breathing thick air again. Faces sun-bronzed around white-raccoon eye circles created by the shade of our glacier glasses, we felt immeasurably lighter in mid-troposphere, ready to perform cartwheels while sharing familiar jokes.

"What are the three notable attributes of a Denali climbing veteran?" I asked the still-unsmiling Tomato.

"High pain threshold, bad memory," he answered, "and, uhhh, I forget the third."

The next morning, I awoke to blinding sunlight reflecting off the glacier, roaring ski-plane engines, and a splitting headache. It would be my closest brush with high-altitude symptoms for the entire trip.

As I crawled out of the tent, a raven peered at me with eerie acumen from a block of snow, cocking its head doglike. I closed my eyes, took a deep breath, and when I looked again he was gone.

Protected from the unforgiving sun under a shade umbrella, perched in a lawn chair, I wrote in my journal about the hundreds of climbers we had spoken to; 1,126 of these pilgrims would follow the hero's path up Denali this summer. Like most years, more than half of them reached the South Summit. Statistics now show that the majority of modern-day attempts are made by clients having their trails broken and their meals cooked by devoted, Karstens-style guides. Another sad new trend over the last two decades shows that climbers are now increasingly content with tackling the easiest route—the west buttress—in order to tag the highest point on the continent, and then leave, as quickly as possible. There are still Archdeacons, Lloyds, and Cooks drawn to Denali, if only because mountaineering often attracts the narcissistic, ego-driven personality—particularly on the challenging routes. But times are now changing. In 2016, fewer than fifty climbers attempted the more difficult climbs, including only seven up the once-popular Muldrow Glacier. No one reached the North Peak.

Relative to the unknown and incredibly advanced terrain that the Sourdoughs confronted more than a century ago, climbers repeated a few technically difficult routes on Denali and the neighboring Mt. Foraker. But all of these climbs were variations, solos, or speed ascents of earlier established routes. In other words, the pioneering era is long gone on North America's highest peaks.

I flew out of the Alaska Range for the last time in a Twin Otter aircraft. This elongated plane carried eight hundred pounds of gear strapped behind seven unwashed bodies in sweat-stiffened clothing behind one clean-shaven pilot wishing for nose plugs. Overjoyed to be leaving the sterile, cold glaciers, we ogled the greenery and running water below as if hallucinating, our cameras winking at the verdancy. The pilot, for his part, would be happy just to get us out of his plane and begin spraying the air freshener.

He threw out our gear to us on the tarmac in Talkeetna—a drinking town with a climbing problem—a half an hour later. If we were pioneers walking and boating out more than a hundred miles, it would've taken a week.

That night in the Fairview Inn, over obligatory loud music and arm curling exercises, it was plain to see that I lacked training, even though the last month had suffused me with new energy. I had to go to this local pub if only because the camaraderie and storytelling closure embodies today's Denali climbing culture—just as McPhee's Saloon in Fairbanks did a century ago. Unfortunately, I hadn't placed any bets about reaching the summit.

I returned home charged up about solving the Sourdough mystery. After posting on forums, making dozens of phone calls and researching park service records for climbers who had tackled the Sourdough Couloir, the route appeared to be unrepeated. In addition to its remoteness, climbers pass by the route because of their focus on reaching the higher South Summit on the opposite side of the Harper Glacier. The more I probed, the 1910 climb only seemed all the more unlikely.

I combed the mountaineering literature for clues, but only turned up the same old mythology about the Sourdoughs. I unearthed hundreds of newspaper articles, discarding the editorialized stories that characterized most early-twentieth-century journalism. Instead, I clung to red-herring interviews of the infamous Lloyd, snippets of mining news about Anderson and Taylor, or the still-alive yet aged Oregon family's remembrances of McGonagall—who lived out of a single suitcase, but was always impeccably dressed in a suit, until he died in their basement room of a heart attack.

Ken Karstens, the great grandson of Harry, the Seventy-Mile Kid, steered me to brief mentions of McGonagall in the 1943 book *Alaska Diary*. Its author, the anthropologist Ales Hrdlicka, hired "McGonigal" as a river companion twenty-one years after the climb. Hrdlicka had been taken with his view of Denali, rising above the river mists, but completely overlooked the accomplishments of his elderly, cranky, Irish-blooded guide who safely escorted him for weeks through the wilderness to study native villagers. If McGonagall—constantly tinkering with and repairing the boat's engine—had seen fit to mention his climb, Hrdlicka would've disregarded it as yet another of the many myths he had heard from other senior Sourdoughs with "bad memories" along the riverbanks.

This epitomizes the challenge of understanding the Sourdoughs. Like Service's fictional protagonist Sam McGee enjoying the red-hot furnace, or Yako using his magic to turn an ocean wave into Denali, the actual accomplishments of the northern pioneers and Cheechakos alike have been either forgotten or reassembled into a post-modern version of the Sacred Story: Cook's *To the Top of the Continent*, Jack London's *Call of the Wild*, or Lloyd's *New York Times* account.

Following Cook's trail, Lloyd somehow received most of the credit for the climb. Even in death, he became the only member of the 1910 team who received a lengthy obituary. While the Fairbanks Pioneers of Alaska have restored Taylor and Lloyd's gravestones, the names and dates on the tombstones in the Sitka Pioneer Cemetery are so faded that the officials there don't know exactly where Anderson's remains lie. McGonagall, behind the scenes throughout both life and death, was cremated. If someone knows where the bachelor's ashes settled, I couldn't find them.

After months of further research for a magazine article, I came to understand how the Sourdoughs might have performed the climb but not whether they actually completed it. So right up until my deadline loomed, the article remained a myth-busting.

On a whim, I revisited the design of their creepers, which may have been more like modern crampons. In 1932, Grant Pearson's park service expedition that dealt with the crevasse deaths found two pairs of the 1910 creepers on the Muldrow Glacier. Since the Sourdoughs had no intention of climbing another mountain they had discarded them on "Wall Street" below McGonagall Pass. Even more than eighty years ago, the rangers saw these creepers as valuable artifacts and brought them out to be displayed in a museum.

Two months after my Denali climb, I flew to Georgia to examine the creepers under a glass case shared by a bust of Abe Lincoln at the Atlanta International Airport. Part of a Centennial National Park Service exhibit, the nine pointers were still sharp and free of rust. They were 107 years old and had sat on the glacier for 22 years.

Further research revealed that, after the Sourdoughs' climb, hob-nailed boots and the small, four-pointed creepers that Browne's team used in 1912 remained the only tools for step-chopping English and American climbers until mid-century. This old chopping tradition prevailed despite a ten-point, heavy-steel crampon that the English climber and engineer Oscar Eckenstein had invented for use in the European Alps. Eckenstein, who preferred climbing unroped, had introduced a new technique of "balance climbing," rather than the former ponderous, brute-force technique of cutting hundreds of steps up mountainsides. After strapping these on in 1908, Eckenstein ditched hobnailed boots and primitive creepers and never chopped a step again.

Eckenstein's story and a diagram of his crampons appeared in an obscure Austrian Alpine Club newsletter that same year, published in German and inaccessible to the Sourdoughs. The crampons were only sold in Europe, but not until 1913. English and American climbers shunned both the crampons and the eccentric Eckenstein—despite their mention in the 1920 classic technique book *Mountaincraft*.

Now I began to wonder if Lloyd had not been exaggerating about their "creepers." These unique nine-pointers could have given the Sourdoughs the needed edge to get up and down their final, steep gully.

Excited, I pulled up the interviews of Lloyd telling different reporters about this vital piece of gear. "McGonagle [*sic*] invented a new kind of ice creeper," Lloyd told the *Seattle Times* after their climb in 1910. "It is one that covers the entire sole of the foot. If it hadn't been for these creepers, and the fact that we carried files with us to keep them sharp we never could have climbed up the steep slopes."

At this, I caught my breath. Climbers didn't sharpen their crampons for decades, until guides began tackling steep ice in Europe.

"With these creepers a man can scale an almost perpendicular wall," Lloyd finished. "Had we been equipped with the ordinary ice creepers we couldn't have climbed half way."

If the *Times* had been based in the European Alps, or if American mountaineering weren't such an obscure sport practiced by eccentric clubbers and cloaked in inscrutable terminology, the reporter might have asked Lloyd to expand upon their crampon-climbing technique.

Then I returned to the interview of Taylor, whom Kantishna miners called "Honest Bill." He told Norman Bright: "We took our . . . creepers and walked right over everything and forgot about steps." In other words, because of their innovative crampons, they didn't *need* steps—all of which explained how they could have climbed such a steep gully so quickly.

These crampons could explain everything: somehow, in far-off Alaska, a total neophyte climber—who happened to be a methodical tinkerer—ingeniously came up with an even better design than the British engineer-alpinist. McGonagall's galvanized crampons were lighter and provided a platform that added stiffness, which provided security on steep slopes (otherwise missing with floppy moccasins). McGonagall had unknowingly anticipated the future game of ice climbing, which would stall in this country for a half century after the Sourdough climb, until Americans finally brought back more innovative tools and techniques from the Alps.

McGonagall's winter journeys across frozen rivers and up steep slopes would have inspired the design. With these revolutionary crampons, Anderson, McGonagall, and Taylor could have climbed the steeps without steps. They could have bent their ankles and "flat-footed," effectively using what would later be called French technique—saving the time-consuming, creeper-footed process of chopping steps like Karstens and Browne and all the other climbers did until the 1970s on Denali.

As for the inexperience of the Sourdoughs, they weren't the only dilettante climbers in North America getting away with murder, particularly in the early days of ice climbing. In 1930, two inexperienced Yale students "stole" the first ascent of Pinnacle Gully on New Hampshire's Mt. Washington from under the noses of experienced Harvard and upperclassmen Yale climbers. Like the Sourdoughs with Cook, these Yalies were spurred on by competition. And through an act of creative imagination, they were able to tackle the climb largely because they lacked the knowledge of more seasoned climbers intimidated by the dangers and difficulties of the five-hundred-foot-high, water-ice gully. These beginners—Julian Whittlesey and Sam Scoville—quickly knocked off the climb that would remain New England's test piece for decades. They climbed it on a bitter, subzero February day.

More than fifty years later, when asked whether Pinnacle Gully also remained his hardest climb, Whittlesey replied, "It was the only one." Asked why he stopped climbing, like Billy Taylor, he replied, "Can't say I really got started."

With the same lack of fear, a pinch of ignorance, the competitive desire to beat out the Cheechakos, and their futuristic crampons, I realized their 1910 climb could have been possible as an act of creative imagination. But needing more, vying for a conclusion, I turned to reexamining Parker and Browne's expedition.

Clearly, the step-chopping efforts that Browne described in their repeated summit attempts wouldn't have been necessary if they wore more advanced crampons. Even the *Mountaincraft* book recommended that creepers with fewer than six spikes weren't worth carrying. So shod, Browne and company's traditional mountaineering backgrounds made them move slowly and conservatively up the mountain. If they had been moving more securely—hence faster—up the final summit slope, without laboriously chopping every step, they would have beaten the storm that turned them back. Better gear and less experience, in this case, would have been to their advantage: they would have easily finished the last few hundred yards to the highest South Peak before Karstens's Alaskan party knocked it off the next year.

Browne, Parker, or LaVoy couldn't spot the Sourdough flagpole in 1912. But they carried two cameras, including a state-of-the-art three-by-five-inch Graflex that LaVoy, a professional photographer, had obtained from the National Geographic Society.

On the advice of my friend and fellow Sourdough skeptic, Brian Okonek, who had thoroughly researched the 1912 expedition, I turned to the Belmore Browne papers and photographs archived at Dartmouth College. Among the files, Okonek identified a large negative shot by LaVoy, the expedition photographer—Browne's smaller Kodak camera images lacked the resolution of the larger Graflex camera.

LaVoy found an intriguing viewpoint from eighteen thousand feet on the eastern or South Peak side of the Harper Glacier. With his camera he captured a scene looking 1.75 miles across the glacier (he didn't know that he was focusing on the Sourdough Couloir and the rocky outcroppings that supposedly held the flagpole). From that distance, none of the 1912 climbers would have seen the mythical pole with their naked eye. Even with the binoculars, they would have been hard pressed to find it because they didn't know—even generally—where to focus on the north side of the continent's biggest mountain. Amid their own hunt for the summit, they could hardly be expected to verify someone else's passage. Besides, the 1912 trio was suffering from the cold, the altitude, and stomach cramps caused by their diet of sickly sweet, fatty pemmican meat. So LaVoy simply exposed this spectacular skyline as a compelling, black-and-white scenic picture. He fired off at least two more photographs by rotating the camera, thinking that the images could be stitched together for a panorama.

Off the mountain, defeated, they returned to family life and their careers as artist and filmmaker (La Voy came back in 1932 and recovered Theodore Koven's body on the Muldrow Glacier). He gave the images he shot from eighteen thousand feet to Browne. Since the photographs were not selected for his *Conquest of McKinley* book, for the last century, these three pieces of the panoramic puzzle have scarcely been touched.

On a hunch, following Okonek's advice, I scanned the old photograph that showed the Sourdough Couloir. Okonek and I then used computers never dreamed of by the pioneers so that we could, in effect, zoom in to this high-resolution image and transport ourselves to the top of the couloir in 1912. By magnifying in 400 percent, we discovered a vertical pole-like object contrasted against a snowfield and surrounded by pixelated-looking summit shale of the same tonality.

This dark vertical line extends from a rock outcrop right where the Sourdoughs would have logically planted their pole: at the top of the couloir and on the skyline of the ridge so that it might be seen with a distant telescope. Careful examination of the entire photograph did not reveal any other vertical lines, nor any other straight lines matching that of a spruce tree cut from the forest below. The object itself has light falling on the right side and a shadow on the left, congruous with the lighting on other terrain features, and the object unnaturally extends above the skyline—unlike any other feature in the entire photograph.

There's nothing like this object anywhere else in the image. Just to be sure, I shared the photo with several professional photographers and an image-analysis researcher. They all concluded that the line (or pole) is not a scratch. And no one could say that the Graflex camera wouldn't be able to resolve an object at that distance. It stands like a tree, highlighted against the sky, seventeen thousand feet above timberline.

I felt exhilarated. I looked again: at the top of the blustery couloir, in the final rocks needed to shore down the heavy limbed spruce, the pole is right where the 1913 climbers described seeing it the next year. Their strongest climber described it, in flowing script, in his journal: "I saw it standing out against the blue sky," Walter Harper wrote, "The pole was about twelve or fourteen feet long."

To put myself in the moccasins of these 1913 climbers, I reread their journals alongside the photograph. Stuck's diary, which I'd never read until now, clinched it:

> *Much discredit has been thrown on this exploit, largely due to the foolish conduct of the men themselves, and the thing is very generally disbelieved. While we sat there, Walter cried: "I see the flagpole", pointing to a peak just below the highest point of the great N. ridge. Then Karstens saw it, and getting out the field glasses it stood out plain and unmistakable to all. It has weathered the storms of three years, and I am very much pleased indeed to be able to carry down confirmation of the exploit of Taylor and Anderson (not Lloyd). We had proposed all along, if time and weather served, climbing the N. peak after reaching the summit of the S, the higher eminence, in order to verify or disprove the planting of the pole. This will not now be necessary: all four of us have seen the staff still standing.*

It all suddenly made sense. For them to have fictionalized their journals to assure that both peaks of Denali remained an "all-Alaskan climbed mountain" now felt like a half-baked conspiracy theory.

Without further ado, I revised my myth-busting magazine story into a celebration of the Sourdoughs. I felt relieved. The lengthy piece included the zoomed-in portion of the photograph unveiling the infamous flagpole.

This image says it all. Although I briefly lost faith, my "god" once again became more real to me than the one described in Psalms, Exodus, or Deuteronomy. I had not climbed alone because my heroes had broken the trail and showed how the geography of my fears—despite all of the past failures—could be mapped into a realistic quest.

Looking at the picture, I can imagine the trio cursing at one another there at 18,500 feet, stomping their moccasin-cramponed feet to stay warm, while they took turns chopping a fifteen-inch-deep hole in the ice with the hatchet. McGonagall sat in the snow watching, panting, too sick to help. With great care not to drop it, Anderson and Taylor lifted the pole vertically and planted it into the hole—stacking a couple-foot-high pyramid of rocks to secure its base— as the highest white spruce above the sea of spruce forests throughout the North. With the hatchet they cut their hank of cotton rope into four guylines and tied them halfway up the pole out to surrounding spurs of black shale. In deference to their sponsors, the hulk-shouldered Taylor then used the flat edge of their hatchet to nail a board onto the pole where it protruded from the snow. Down at tunnel camp, certain of their success, they had inscribed the board with their names, those of their sponsors, and the date. Taylor hammered the nails into the wood one at a time, slowly, as if taking part in a solemn ritual, careful not to accidentally hit or nail his hand into the wood through the fur mitten. Then they tied on the huge flag, which hung limp on the kind of crystalline, still day made for climbing such a high peak. They would make history, showing the world—while inspiring others to follow in their footsteps—what anyone could do, regardless of age and experience if you put your heart into it.

Charlie McGonagall, nearly incapacitated by altitude illness, beckoned the other two to go on without him. He would later tell his friend Harry Karstens that he was afraid that if he climbed any higher he wouldn't make it back down. The important thing in his mind was that he'd done his part and taken his turn shouldering the pole up the steep hill. It's not hard to see his suffering even though he would never speak about it in his later years. He laid down next to the pole in crusted snow with his arms out straight and his mitted palms held up to the sky and put his head back, worried about his nosebleed. Eventually he sat up, unable to bear the cold any longer. Then he turned down the daunting and steep gully, facing forward as he carefully kicked his ingenious crampons into the deep snow steps they'd booted out on their way up. At hard snow and ice patches he faced outward and flexed his ankles in the floppy moccasins and flat-footed down—fully engaging all nine points of his crampons. One slip and the fall would've killed him. As America's first ice climber, he focused carefully and balance climbed, invested in each step, stomping in firmly while he nursed a splitter headache. It was nerve-racking work, but he had survived worse caught out on mail runs in subzero blizzards without snowshoes or shelter. He would wait for his friends down at Tunnel Camp.

Unaffected by the altitude—thanks to their fast ascent and repeated acclimatization trips up Karstens Ridge—Billy and the Swede then raced one another the last mile and nine hundred feet up the narrow ridge to the North Peak. It was thirty degrees below zero. Aside from this triumphant moment, their lives, even their personalities, have been all but lost to history.

"The old timers are not mentioned," Harry Karstens said specifically about Anderson and Taylor reaching the peak. "Such is life for those who accomplish things but have no influence." Yet while climbing Denali, they influenced me, immensely, and now I can imagine them as never before.

On top, they shook hands. As the Swede told Grant Pearson, they "whooped" with joy, howling as pagans into the top of the troposphere. Since they'd never climbed a mountain before, as taciturn frontiersmen, both were surprised, yet careful, to hide the swell of emotions that came over them. Taylor caught himself feeling *light-like* from the altitude, wondering whether his feet would *come up on him.*

They looked down over a sea of clouds with only the summit of Mt. Foraker sticking through the undercast like Yako's penultimate white wave. The sun shone above them and even with its distant lie of warmth, the solid white cloud layer below served as an immense reflector that illuminated them in bright, coruscating light—highlighting their ascension. Neither miner had any interest in photography, so Anderson kept the Kodak camera in his rucksack. After all, their mitts were iced over and *it was colder than hell.* Since they no longer needed the heavy coal shovel for digging steps, they plunged it into the summit as a marker. Caribou fur from their sleeping pads the night before clung to their black-and-white-striped parkas sewn from mattress covers.

I like to believe, while they stood gobstruck on top, that they felt as I did. We thought that by pushing past our limits we were on an outward, physical journey, as if to vouchsafe our own strength, but once on top we found humility and our place in the world. We had found a stillness within, our church replete with a god.

The two climbers crept back down with crampons crunching into their knife blade ridge. It took them less than an hour to reach the top of the couloir. At the flagpole monument, they nervously chewed sourdough donuts and guzzled the last of the now-chilled cocoa from Thermos bottles as they psyched themselves up for the most difficult part of the descent. Then they turned down the steep gully, focused on each step. Focused on their survival. Profiled against the cobalt sky above hung the sagging stars and stripes on a spruce tree, stuck into the cresting wave of Denali. All of this epic was no more a myth—the people of Yako would say about their Sacred Story—than Raven's giant spear from the Distant Time. It stood just as Billy Taylor had pictured it all from below in the forest.

INDEX

Hamilton, Jeff, xxiv, xxviii, xxix, 107–109, 111

Happy Birthday, during 2016 Denali expedition, xxvi–xxvii

Harper, Walter, x, 75–81, 85, 122

Harper Basin, xxvii

Harper Glacier, xix, xxvii, xxviii, 62, 81–83, 92–94, 114; South Peak of, 44, 55, 100, 104, 120

Harper Icefall, 5

Heavyweights of Fairbanks, 35

high-altitude acclimatization, xix, xxi, 125

hoax rumors, about Cook 1906 expedition, 22–25, 26, 40, 51–54

horses, during 1903 expedition, 10, 13, 16, 19–20

Hrdlicka, Ales, 114–15

humility, 86, 126

Hutchins, Michael, 107, 109–110

Ikeda, Masayuki, cerebral edema of, 110–11; death of, 111; at Denali Pass, 110; helicopter rescue attempt of, 111

incapacitation, of McGonagall, 123–24

Inman, Cory, xxiv, xxix, 60, 107, 109, 111

Inuit, 53

Italian Duke of Abruzzi, 74, 76

January, 1911: Lloyd interview, 67–68; McGonagall, 67–68

Joiner, Bill, 93–94

journals, 7, 51–52, 81–82

Juneau, 89

Kahiltna Glacier, xvii

Kantishna: Cook relating to, 15, 29; Lloyd relating to, 29, 35, 38, 40–41, 43, 89; mining district of, ix, xx, 3, 23, 25, 58, 70, 72, 75, 118; Taylor in, 101

Kantishna River, 55

Karstens, Harry, 73, 124; background of, 74–75; as "The Seventy-Mile Kid," x, 75, 80–81, 83, 88

Karstens, Ken, 114–15

Karstens Ridge, 62, 82, 90, 93–94, 99; in Lloyd Sourdough expedition, 3, 43, 45

Karstens-Stuck expedition, 1913, 87; Anderson relating to, 75, 86, 88; conflict during, 79–80; creepers used during, 68, 70, 75, 79–81, 83–84, 99, 100; expedition-style climbing strategy for, 74; flagpole seen by, 122–23; Harper in, x, 75–81, 85, 122; McGonagall relating to, 75–76; preparation for, 73; Sourdough accomplishment of, 82; sourdough starter with, 76; Tatum in, 75–77

Acknowledgments

For Elizabeth Kaplan, my literary agent, who believed in me when the story seemed unlikely to fly, you gave this book wings. Thank you.

Looking back three dozen years I am also indebted to the park service—in particular, all of the staff at the Talkeetna Ranger Station and at Denali National Park headquarters—for initially hiring me in 1982, then covering my expenses as a volunteer during the final tour of duty in the summer of 2016. For too many partners to name on and around the mountain since 1976, this book is written with you in mind. Most recently, my regrets to Ranger Bob Tomato, Michael Hutchins, Bobby Cosker, Justin Fraser, Jeff Hamilton, and Cory Inman in case my observations strayed far from theirs while up on the mountain; in my mind our trip remains a stellar example of mountaineering camaraderie and teamwork. My appreciation also remains boundless for the men and women of the Department of the Interior who have served, and in some instances given their lives, on the mountain.

I am thankful to Brian Okonek, formerly of Alaska-Denali Guiding, who hired me so many years ago. Then more recently, he tipped me off with leads about the Sourdoughs, and finally, gave this manuscript a proofread and made corrections that no other reader, mountaineer, or historian would have caught.

To David and Aisha Stevenson: thanks for the ride and ongoing Alaska hospitality. Stateside, Alison Osius and Duane Raleigh, my editors at *Ascent*, kindly allowed (and fixed) my original Denali-sized, book-inspiring article, "The Donut Eaters," which became "The Sourdough Enigma," published in the spring of 2017. And to Lynn Aliya, my sounding board and reader as the idea all came together.

I am also grateful for the support of, David Loftus, Ted Loftus, Ann Younger, Ken and Eugene Karstens, Tom Falley, Roger Robinson, Mark Westman, Laura Waterman, Jed Williamson, Gary Kofinas, Beth Selzer, Daniel Osborne, Steve Swenson, Andy Hall, Daryl Miller, Bill Rotecki, Bill Joiner, Patricia Schmidt, Jeff Babcock, and Lou Dawson. I would like to thank the attorney, film agent, famous actor who read the audio version, and administrative-assistant typist—but since these people don't exist, I will thank my most faithful and aged companion. Jax laid patiently as I spent endless hours writing, rewriting, reading, deleting, and then rewriting again. When I could take no more, Jax encouraged me to run with him, often uphill, where all my best ideas sprang forth—he's only a rescue dog, but without him I might've been lost. Otherwise, salvation from the countless hours of home-office isolation were somewhat relieved by working at a corner table in town—thank you Bonfire Coffee.

Finally, for the childless, long-deceased, yet skookum, husky sonsofagun Sourdoughs Billy Taylor, Pete Anderson, and Charlie McGonagall—thanks for the inspiration. I'm still riding downhill without using the brakes.